Wings
of Change

The inside story of Australia's first
female Green Beret Commando
and her fight for change

Robyn
Fellowes

Wings of Change

Copyright © Robyn Fellowes

First published 2022

ISBN: 978-0-6456776-0-7   Paperback

ISBN: 978-0-6456063-9-3   E-book

All rights reserved. Without limiting the rights under copyright reserved above, no part of this publication may be reproduced, stored in or introduced into a database and retrieval system or transmitted in any form or by any means (electronic, mechanical, photocopying, recording or otherwise) without the prior written permission of the owner of the copyright.

Illustrations reproduced with permission.

Editing, layout and cover design by Meg Hatfield

Printed in Australia

DEDICATION

This book is dedicated to my Mum.
Her enormous strength, resilience and faith in the face of constant adversity was something to behold.
Mum taught me do the right thing, to make change and help people who could not help themselves.
Thank you Mum.

ACKNOWLEDGEMENTS

Being able to write and publish this book in less than six months was due to making myself accountable to a willing friend for my milestones. I surrounded myself with a team of people who all brought their skills, knowledge and creativity to the writing process. I was never afraid to ask for help.

I was told that writing a book is about who you become at the end of the process, and that is so true. I would like to thank those friends and colleagues who willingly came on this journey with me.

To my mentor Sandra Musgrave, who told me at the start that the key to writing was always describing - where you are, when it is happening and who you are with – and I kept that in mind from day one. When I was about half way through I told Sandra that I had a gut full of writing and was quitting, she said, 'The fun has finished. This is when the hard work starts!' And she was right. I'm still not quite sure where to put the verbs, but my grammar has improved immensely.

To Sharyn Fewster, who wanted to be called Mentor, with a capital M, thank you for forcing me to 'get raw' with my emotions, as hard as that was.

To Meg Hatfield, my editor and designer, who grilled me like the CIA to make sure those emotions ended up in ink, thank you. Meg gave me permission to put in exclamation marks and worked with me hour upon hour, to make sense of my stories.

To Kerryn Fewster, official Head of the Manuscript Review Team, your input was always insightful and a much-needed civilian point of view. You did what you said you were going to, and the book is infinitely better because of your contribution.

To Chris Robinson who was there from the start, who gave me a male perspective and who helped me remove my own biases to ensure the book was balanced. Thank you, Chris.

To Kath Stewart, who reviewed an early version of the manuscript and honestly told me, 'You have a lot of work to do to turn this into a book'. Thank you Kath. You were right!

To Karen Sander who held me accountable from the start, frequently confiscating my phone and allowing me to focus without distraction. Thank you for your persistence.

To Dr Dee Gibbon, who put up with my text stalking, and under the condition that I would stop stalking her, helped me turn my timeline of events into a story. Thank you.

To my family and close friends who fielded my many questions and took the time to help me remember, my thanks to you all.

Finally, to the amazing women I have worked with around the world, I wish you all the best as you strive to better your countries and communities in the face of adversity – being the agents of change your countries need you to be.

FOREWORD
by Colonel Amanda Fielding (Retired)

I knew of Robyn long before I met her. It was 1998 and I was a Lieutenant posted to Townsville, Queensland. I was an enthusiastic young officer at the beginning of my career, full of hope and opportunity. Robyn, and two other women officers, were the talk of this military garrison town. They were the first women ever to be permitted to attempt the Commando selection course and we were all watching very closely to see how they would perform.

My female colleagues and I were eager for these women to prove that women can undertake roles in the combat Corps. Such a feat would open doors for women throughout the military to enter combat roles and have other gender restrictions removed or, at least, reconsidered. There was a lot riding on the shoulders of these three women.

The fact that all three women passed the selection course under such close scrutiny, is a tribute to their characters as well as their physical prowess. I recall at the time, that the focus was very much placed on their physicality and ability to meet the physical standards of the selection course. All I knew of Robyn at the time, was that everyone referred to her as the 'Amazonian' woman - tall, blonde, attractive and naturally athletic.

You would think that a woman with a reputation such as this was the exception to the norm, and that her achievements would be difficult for others to live up to, and that you couldn't possibly relate to such a woman. I certainly did. I shamefully admit to having this bias. However, as you embark on reading Robyn's story, you will find that this is not the case and that Robyn is incredibly human, as well as being an incredible human being.

Yes, she is athletic and physically fit. However, much of her physical successes can be attributed to her determination and training but moreover, her incredible mental resilience and self-belief. This is not to say she has not had knocks and falls along the way. She has. She has had highs and lows like the rest of us, set-backs, times of despair, and of being overwhelmed to a point of hopelessness. It is how she has dealt with these tough times since childhood, that is admirable and I believe something we can all learn from, whether you are in the military or not.

I finally met Robyn when I was deployed to Afghanistan in 2015 as the Gender Advisor. Robyn headed the Assessment team for the Resolute Support Headquarters. As the Gender Advisor Cell was relatively new (it was originally set up under the International Security Force), Robyn and her team were keen to learn how we planned on conducting our role, given the constraints and cultural beliefs surrounding Afghan women in the military and police. Robyn was so keen, she assigned herself to my team as our assessment officer.

I immediately liked Robyn. As you could imagine, I was curious to meet this legendary female green beret, that I had heard so much about. Even though we had numerous mutual friends who told me what a great person she was and that she had a wicked sense of humour, I still had this perception / bias that she would be masculine, and one of those super competitive women.

Not only was Robyn warm and very, very funny, she had a genuine passion for others and in the case of Afghanistan, a genuine concern and desire to assist the women in the country to secure a better future for themselves. As such, I asked Robyn if she would like to assist my team with some workshops with women in the Afghan National Army. Our work together grew from there.

Robyn and I made a great team. I was over the moon that life circumstances meant that she was available to come and work for me in Canberra to set up the operational Gender Advisor capability for the Australian Defence Force. The job not only required qualified operational planners, but also required people who had operational credibility and were good human beings. I required uniformed members with a humanitarian bent and desire to make the world a better place for men, women, boys and girls. Robyn was definitely one of these people.

There will be stories contained within this book that you will relate to, as Robyn describes her time both inside and outside the military. You will also undoubtedly relate to those sliding door moments that we all have in our lives; the choices we make, the choices that are sometimes made for us. These choices either halt us in the path that we are on, or can set us on a new course. At the end of the day, Robyn highlights the importance of making your own life choices while staying true to yourself and your beliefs. She also highlights that we all have a choice in how we react and respond to what life throws at us. That change can be hard and it can be good, even when we don't choose it.

When I think of Robyn, I think of the quote by Nelson Mandela, the ultimate humanitarian; "I learnt that courage was not the absence of fear, but the triumph over it". There is no doubt that Robyn has triumphed and shown great courage, honesty and generosity in sharing her story with us.

CONTENTS

The need for change	2
Shaped for change	7
My road to change	21
Joining the Army	26
Changing up	37
Time to step up	46
Women talk to women	50
Going Commando	62
Not ready for change	73
Missed opportunities	79
An opportunity not missed	84
Why train women?	88
Too much change	94
Initiating change - Women, Peace and Security	102
Change for the family	115
A country in need of change	119
Investment in change	136
Bad change, good change	142
Future change	148

1 – THE NEED FOR CHANGE
Be the change you wish to see in the world – Mahatma Gandhi

My story begins and ends living in Ravensbourne, a picturesque part of Australia, a beautiful, lush and serene rainforest region about 40 kilometres north of Toowoomba on the edge of the Great Dividing Range, in glorious Queensland. Ravensbourne is currently my home - an area surrounded by beautiful trees, towering tallowwoods and blue gums full of bird life. Pretty-face wallabies, dingos and deer roam everywhere. It is very close to where I had the life-changing epiphany that would send me along a new path in my career as an agent of change.

I was driving home to Ravensbourne late one night from Toowoomba. I was exhausted from a long day of running my business. While driving up a hill in Geham, north of Highfields, near the top of the hill, I saw a huge grey gum tree on the left-hand side of the road. It was well known to locals as many young people had 'accidentally' driven into that tree over the years and most had died from their injuries. There were often fresh flowers placed at the base of the tree as a gesture of mourning for the many lives lost. One vibrant young man who I knew quite well was critically injured after driving into the tree and had to reside in a nursing home due to the brain damage he had sustained.

It was while contemplating his fate that my thoughts began

to wander... and I started thinking... maybe his 'accident' wasn't an accident after all. Maybe none of them were. Maybe people had been feeling exactly the way I was feeling right now - disconnected, stressed and terribly tired. My body ached all over. I was living in chronic pain. In that moment, I just wanted all the pain and stress to go away. I kept thinking – I can fix all this right now. I can make the pain go away. Almost subconsciously, but with the same determination that I had pursued everything in my life, my left hand started to apply pressure to the steering wheel, turning my Captiva towards the 'Death Tree'.

I increased the pressure on the accelerator, speeding up, my high beam headlights clearly lighting up the massive white trunk. I was nearly off the road now, both hands clenched on the steering wheel to stay on my target, the Tree of Death. I felt ready to meet my fate and submit to the desire for all my pain to go away. Then, just as suddenly as the dark thoughts had overcome me, they lifted. With only a microsecond to spare, I suddenly veered away from the tree and back onto the road, and in doing so, saved my own life. **WTF** just happened? Now I just wanted to get home.

I had never thought for one moment that I was a person who would ever contemplate committing suicide, but with the benefit of hindsight, perhaps my 'tree' epiphany is not so surprising. It woke me up to my **own** need to change. I had recently left the full-time Army after 22 years of service and, like many veterans, felt quite distanced from the people and organisation that had become my family and home away from home. A military career was all I had known in my adult working life. The camaraderie of the Army was gone - the mateship, the teamwork, the feeling part of something bigger than myself. I was no longer a member of the 'green machine'.

I also think it was fair to say that I had experienced some extreme challenges and life-changing circumstances throughout my life leading up to my moment at the tree. While in the army, I was fortunate to be one of only three women able to pass the physically and mentally gruelling Commando Selection course. I went on to be the first female to complete the suite of Commando Special Forces Training courses and earn the coveted Green Beret. This was in 1999, at a time when Australian women were banned from most combat roles - occupations that were exclusively the domain of men. Many men (and arguably some women) certainly did not want women entering these forbidden bastions of masculinity. Entering an all-male domain and somehow managing to pass one of the world's most arduous courses, which the majority of men ultimately fail, wasn't easy. However, it proved to me what women - myself included - can achieve, given the motivation and the opportunity.

Prior to this, I had also managed to pass Army officer training at the Royal Military College Duntroon, another challenging course, whilst suffering an undiagnosed broken ankle – I walk with a limp to this day. As well as the physical challenges of Army service, I saw and experienced things during my multiple military tours of duty that would linger in my psyche, long after the tour had ended.

I had also survived a traumatic childhood defined by a violent father who physically and mentally abused our family over a period of many years. Perhaps I was motivated by my need for my violent father's approval and desire to bring peace to our home. Perhaps fuelled by my natural athletic prowess and innate competitiveness, I had also successfully competed in the upper echelons of athletics. This could have been my professional career if I had made different choices.

I was and remain physically and mentally tough, but on that day on the road, it had all become too much. For a very brief moment I no longer wanted to be here. I'll never really know exactly why, at that particular moment, I felt the need to end my own life or why I somehow managed not to!

What I do know is that this was one of many 'slidng door' moments which have shaped the woman and agent of change that I have become. My story is one of overcoming adversity, helping others and driving positive change. I've been called many things in my life - 'Amazon Woman', 'GI Jane', 'Trail Blazer' - but I've never really considered myself to be any of these things. Other terms used to describe me resonate more deeply: role model, mentor, friend, mate, sister and aunty.

It is my desire to make the world a better place which has inspired me to finally write this book, after many years of pleading by my friends and colleagues. My hope is that readers of this book feel encouraged to overcome whatever adversity or hurdles they may be facing. This may be escaping a violent relationship or home, managing acute physical and psychological pain, coping with unwelcome change, entering a sphere almost entirely dominated by men, or dominated by others who differ from themselves in another significant way.

I hope those contemplating ending their lives, particularly veterans, consider that those moments of acute darkness are never an enduring state. There is always, always hope of a brighter future, even in your darkest hour. Things **do** change!

This book is inspired by my mother, who in her own quiet and determined way, faced extreme adversity and survived. This threat came from within her own home, which should have been a safe haven from the outside world. Despite this she was a tower of strength, mentally and spiritually. She lifted herself above her circumstances and showed my sisters and me that we could be whoever we wanted to be. She taught me that people's past does not define them. She gave me the desire to change things that weren't right – to help people who could not help themselves, people like my Mum. She inspired me to be the best person I can be and the best agent of change I can be.

After my father passed away, my mother finally found peace, if only for the last two years of her life. I only wish that this peaceful period had lasted longer. This book is dedicated to her. I love you, Mum.

2 – SHAPED FOR CHANGE

Throughout my childhood I saw my mother suffer. Her experiences - a new life in a new country, speaking a new language and immensely challenged by my father's violent actions - all shaped the woman I became. She was vulnerable and needed someone to stand up and protect her. As a child I was unable to do this, but it fuelled my desire to stand up for people who cannot protect themselves.

My mother, Helene, was born in Nikolajewka, Bessarabia, Russia in 1939, prior to the start of the Second World War. Bessarabia is now divided between modern-day Moldova and Ukraine. My mother's family was one of many German communities that were allowed to prosper under Catherine the Great's Russian Colonisation Policy. Bessarabia Germans lived there for five or six generations. My mother said to me, 'Russia wanted the Germans there because we were hardworking.'

The German colonists' prosperity was based on many things. They had a Christian faith, were compassionate and hardworking and held virtues such as honesty, humility and thrift. They thrived away from the oppression and hunger crisis being experienced in their homeland. There have continued to be historic and cultural links between the citizens of Moldova and Ukraine and the descendants of the German settlers, like my mother.

In the 1940s when the Russian Red Army forces invaded Bessarabia and then Germany occupied Poland, my mother's family had to flee at very short notice. German soldiers were blowing up the bridges behind them as they tried to slow the Russian advance and protect these refugees. Mum, the second youngest of ten siblings, remembers throwing a tantrum, as she had to leave her doll behind in Poland. She was blissfully unaware that her family had been forced to move with only two hours' notice, to stay ahead of the advancing Russian Army. They needed to get back to the safety of Germany. The Russian Army back then, like today, was not known for its humanitarian regard - rather the opposite. Fleeing was the correct approach if you did not want to end up dead or a prisoner in Siberia!

Mum, (sitting on front of carriage) and her family. Her older brothers had been sent to the Russian Front.

Mum's three older brothers, my uncles who were only young men, were killed in this dreadful war as they fought on the Russian Front. One was Luftwaffe (Air Force), one was a Panzer (Tank) driver and one was a Panzer Grenadier (Motorised Infantry). After the war Mum's mother, my Oma, was told by the local villagers she should get over losing three sons in the war. Oma promptly retorted, 'Well how about I cut off three of your fingers and see how you get over that!'

Mum's family settled in a small village called Untersontheim, Schwabisch Hall, Baden-Wurttemberg, Germany, and are still there today. Life was tough in the aftermath of the war and Mum, seeing her parents struggle to feed many mouths, took it upon herself to make it easier for them. One afternoon on the way home from school when she was in grade seven, about twelve years old, she went to one of the local farmers and asked if she could work in exchange for food and board. He agreed. This was an early example of the immense fortitude, courage and strength Mum displayed her entire life. She gave up her education and left home in order to lessen the burden on her family. I often asked Mum how she achieved this amazing feat at such a young age. Wasn't she scared? Mum would humbly reply, 'I had no choice. I had to do it.'

Several years later Mum had started nursing training in a local hospital when she was devasted by her Dad being rushed to the same hospital with a sudden fatal heart attack. The children now needed to earn more money so Oma would not lose the family home. Mum and her two sisters, Wanda and Dina, went to work in Switzerland as au pairs for several years, sending money back to Germany. Again, Mum gave up her education and a promising career as a nurse in order to help her mother. Many years later Mum received a small Swiss pension from her time working in Switzerland. She would cheekily say, 'I get a Swiss pension and Margrit (her best friend who was actually Swiss) doesn't.'

After her time in Switzerland, Mum bravely travelled to England to work as an au pair so she could learn English. It was here she met my father, Michael, who had been born in Watford, Hertfordshire, England. He was working on the same farm as Mum after he completed Agricultural College. Mum was smitten. She said she had fallen for a mouth full of teeth - he had a great smile. When she returned to Germany they wrote to each other for two years before they were married.

My parents arrived as immigrants in Sydney in February 1964 on SS CANBERRA after a six-week voyage.

An early portrait of my parents. I can see why Mum fell for the 'mouth full of teeth'.

Mum was pregnant with her 'stow-away daughter' - my eldest sister - and suffered dreadfully from both sea sickness and morning sickness. They travelled as 'Ten Pound Poms'. To do this, Mum had to surrender her German citizenship to get a British passport. In quick succession Mum had courageously given up both her home country and her citizenship. She moved to Australia, where she had to speak a new language she still barely knew.

Business owners came on board SS CANBERRA the day she docked, to check out the new labour force. It must have been like a meat market! The next day Dad and Mum started work - Dad in a tyre factory and Mum as a waitress in a restaurant. The two new immigrants were keen to do anything their new country asked of them. My parents were the only people on the ship's manifest who had 'Department of Immigration' as their point of contact. Everybody else had family or friends in Australia. They must have felt very independent, bravely going it alone. They were put up in a house in Ashfield, an inner west suburb of Sydney, with four other couples. It was cramped, but they had a job and a roof over their heads.

They worked hard in Sydney until, with Dad's parents' financial help, they purchased 88 acres in Highfields, near Toowoomba, Queensland. Dad told me that when he was studying at an Agricultural College back in England, he opened up an atlas at a map of Australia. He pointed to South East Queensland and said that was where he would build a farm and raise his family. And he did! Although I learned to fear my father, I always appreciated the fact I was born in Toowoomba and blessed to have been brought up in such a wonderful, safe and secure part of the world. I did not know just how much Dad would change!

My parents moved onto the land, living in a tent initially while they built a home and established their farm. It was a large fertile block of land, semi cleared, and excellent farming and grazing land. Our farm became a menagerie with a piggery, beef cattle, horses (which we preferred to ride bareback), goats, chickens, bantams, quails, turkeys and a pack of free-loading dogs. Some years later my cousin visiting from Germany thought one of the dogs was called 'Pissoff'. Every time it ran up to us, tail wagging furiously, we would tell it to 'Piss off'!

Enjoying a bare back ride on Pancho.

Early on, life changed drastically for Mum. She found herself isolated from her supportive family. She was an immigrant with four daughters under seven years old. The 'mouth full of teeth' had learnt to bite. Dad became domineering and violent. Mum became a victim of serious domestic violence, suffering both mental and physical abuse. Dad also firmly controlled the finances. There was little or no support for her, either emotionally or financially. Dad blamed Mum for everything and anything that went wrong. If an animal died on the farm for any reason - if a cow died calving or a piglet got squashed by its mother - or he did not have any money, it was all Mum's fault. Mum's approach was the exact opposite.

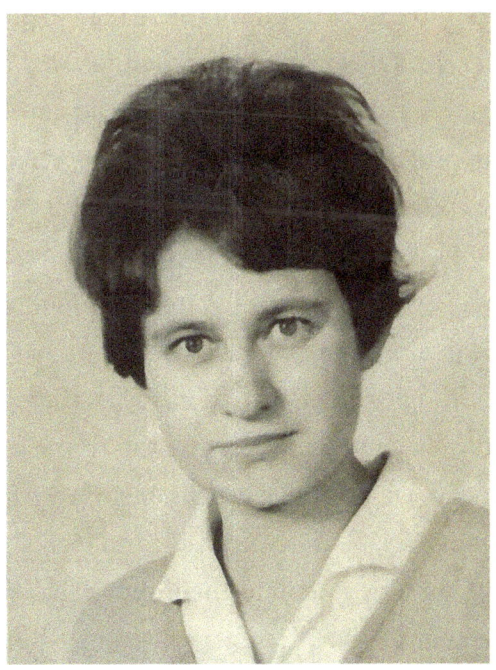

A young woman's determination and resilience on display.

She was always positive and practical. She would say 'Live stock, dead stock!' She knew it was inevitable you would lose animals on a farm. Her pragmatic approach, however, was not shared by Dad and it did not save her from his anger. Mum would be yelled at and then bashed up. Dad was over six feet tall and very strong. I am surprised that she walked away with her life. I often pleaded with her to take us somewhere safe, away from Dad. Mum simply said, 'If I take you away, he will find us and kill me'. What else could she do? I often wondered how much internal strength Mum had to get up every day and move forward. But she did, and we all watched on and learnt to survive too.

My sisters and I were not immune to the violence. Although we tried to look out for each other, we had no defences against his terrible temper. Dad would get angry, grab us by the hair and bang our heads together - giving us the thrashing he apparently thought we deserved. After school one day I found that Mum had crawled into the sanctuary of my bed, bloodied and bruised. She told me, 'I am OK. Please go and put Dad in a good mood'. And that is what we did – every time. We kept Dad in a good mood so there was peace. Then something would go wrong and the abuse would start again. We always walked on eggshells, feeling anxious. Was Dad mad again? Yes, he was. We needed to escape and hide. Running and jumping out of our bedroom windows was our escape route. Our windows regularly became a human waterfall as we piled out to escape the violence. We would run as fast as we could up the paddock until we could no longer hear

Mum's screams of pain.

I would climb my favourite tree for refuge, and wait for the violence to end. The tree had a view of the house, so I could work out when it was safe to go back. I would curl up in the branches, crying, hoping that Mum was all right. Where were my sisters? We usually scattered in different directions, just focused on getting away from the violence. I hoped they were safe too.

Sometimes it would be well into the night before I thought it was safe to climb down and venture back home. Creeping back through the window, listening. Was Dad still in the house? No. A sense of relief would flood over me. Then finding Mum battered and bruised. She was always quiet, even though I could only imagine the pain she would have been suffering. She was so strong, standing at the kitchen sink or by the washing machine trying to get on with her work. I would come up behind her and watch her - just a child wondering how to help her. She would whisper, once again, 'Please just go and put Dad in a good mood'. And we would. We would be the peace makers. Again.

If Mum had access to money maybe we could have left - gone somewhere safe. I heard later there were organisations that could have helped us leave. But Mum did not know about them. I often sat staring at the phone, wanting to dial triple zero, get the police to help Mum and lock Dad up. Back then I knew I was witnessing crimes being committed against my mother. I never called and so the police never came. In hindsight I don't think the police would have done anything. Dad would have punished Mum had I rung. Mum always 'copped it' in the end.

From a young age I began reading self-development books and biographies of successful people. Books from US author Brian Tracy: *No Excuse! The Power of Self-discipline* and Robert Kiyosaki: *Rich Dad Poor Dad. What the rich teach their kids about money – that the poor and middle class do not!* More recently I read books by Brendon Burchard: *The Motivation Manifesto – 9 declarations to claim your personal power*: and *High-Performance Habits – how extraordinary people become that way.* I knew I had to learn from other people's experiences. I abhorred violence. I detested feeling anxious and scared. I dreaded hearing Dad's voice raised in anger. I did not want to repeat my parents' story, or my Mum's life!

My sisters and I were industrious and worked from a young age, on the farm and locally. We wanted to be self-sufficient. We **needed** to be self-sufficient. Mum demonstrated courage, resourcefulness and a good work ethic. We did not realise at the time that these were all traits Mum had displayed at our age. People would say to Mum, 'You have brought your girls up well.' Mum would always say, 'They brought themselves up.' She was forever humble and gracious.

From nine or ten years old, we learnt that we could earn five dollars an hour doing chores for neighbours - picking vegetables, catching chickens, whatever was needed. We learnt that working led to self-sufficiency. We also needed to be mobile, so we learnt to drive cars and ride motorbikes as soon as our feet could reach the pedals or the ground. I was about 12 years old when my little sister and I 'borrowed' Dad's big green Statesman car and I drove it to the Farmers Arms, a pub about five km away along the New England Highway. I was quite tall for my age. I strode confidently into the bar and ordered us a schooner of beer each. Then we sat outside and played Space Invaders. It was illegal on so many levels. Through necessity we had learnt to be resourceful, and to enjoy a beer when we created the chance!

The persona my Dad projected to the world at large was a charming, intelligent, and witty man. He was like two people in one. I used to say he was a psychopath. Not that I knew what a psychopath was, but I think I was pretty close.

Sitting proudly, complete with flares, on my Yamaha 125cc trail bike, which I had bought by saving up the money I earned working at lots of odd jobs.

We were fortunate to be visited by Mum's mother, Oma, and Mum's sister, Tanta (Aunty in German) Wanda, from Germany in the mid 1970s. They were horrified to see how we lived. Mum told me they thought we lived like savages. We certainly looked like savages - wild self-cut hair, hand-me-down clothes, no shoes and red dirty feet from the red soil. It was clearly different from the more refined lifestyles they had in Germany. We did not know any better – it was just how life was.

Dad was on his best behaviour for the three months that Oma and Tanta Wanda lived with us. Dad would call Tanta Wanda 'The General'. I think she was the only woman that Dad respected, so Mum had a reprieve for three months. In true German fashion Tanta Wanda rolled up her sleeves and transitioned our house into a home. She painted it, bought furniture and did what she could to make life easier for Mum. Mum was so very grateful. Her sister did the improvements Mum had wanted, but was not allowed to do. For example, Mum had been secretly saving for a new kitchen table, but Dad found out and took the money.

I enjoyed a visit to Tante Wanda in Germany in 2018 on a break, whilst I was working in South Sudan. I thanked her for making our house a home all those years ago. Like the women I was currently working with in South Sudan, my Mum had just needed a helping hand. It was very emotional for both of us. I believe Tante Wanda had a clear idea of what her sister and nieces had endured in the Land Down Under. I promised Tanta Wanda I would be back to visit her in 2020 and I would practice speaking German so I could talk to her in her native tongue. Sadly, Tante Wanda passed away suddenly in June 2019. I have kept up my daily German practice and will go back to Germany to see the family as soon as I can.

I never understood why Mum stayed with Dad. It must have taken amazing courage and faith. I used to say Mum must have had Stockholm Syndrome, a coping mechanism where people develop positive feelings toward their abusers over time. But despite the abuse, Mum always maintained she loved Dad. She always seemed to have a sense of duty and loyalty to him, although it never appeared to be reciprocated. Mum was incredibly strong, not physically but mentally. After Mum's family visited, they started paying for Mum to visit Germany. However, she would only ever go for two weeks. I asked her later why she did not stay longer. She said Dad always told her to stay in Germany and never come back. Yet she always came back. I cannot think how strong and courageous Mum was to come back to Australia each time, knowing she would endure his hatred all over again.

Mum was a devout Christian and I believe her spiritual faith had a lot to do with her strength and her resolve to stay with Dad. A close family friend told me, 'Yes, Helene was vulnerable, but in her vulnerability, she trusted the Lord implicitly, and her strength was so much greater than her vulnerability. She was the strongest woman I have ever known'. Mum would say to me she had a 'Ring of Fire' protecting her, that believers had a guardian angel protecting them. Mum would have needed a dozen guardian angels! But she did not let the abuse define her. She was kind, gracious and humble with a cheeky sense of humour. She was much loved by all who met her. She reciprocated that love by her incredible generosity. Nobody left our home without something - some avocados, some eggs, some vegetables out of the garden, a piece of carrot cake.

Mum had an incredibly strong German accent. My sisters and I would imitate her in fun, but never in front of her. I once asked why her accent was still so strong, after so many years living in Australia. She said it was because she never learnt to speak English properly. She always had to translate the English to German and back to English in her head, and then say the response. I could not imagine how she did that for over 50 years whilst she dealt with all her other challenges.

Mum consistently demonstrated her quiet resolve, her inner strength and her courage. She was also extremely wise. I would go to her with a problem and she would give me her point of view and then say, 'Just hand your problem over to the Lord. He will sort it out for you'. She was right – I did and He did. Thanks to her I learnt to have faith, be practical and have the courage to do what we thought was right.

However, it was going to take many more years before I would have the courage to confront Dad and challenge him to justify his appalling behaviour towards Mum - and indeed to us all.

3 – MY ROAD TO CHANGE

Although I did not know it at the time, I had already started on the road to change. Throughout my childhood I excelled at athletics. The better I was, the more events I attended, the happier Dad was. Dad was happy. Tick. Therefore, Mum was safe and happy. Tick.

Competing for Highfields State School at a local Sports Day at Goombungee

I competed successfully in numerous Queensland State and National Titles. I won my first National Title in the high jump when I was eight. I was the only student representing Highfields State School at the Queensland All Schools championships. Back then there were only about 60 students at Highfields School. At the opening of the Championships there was me, all on my own, carrying the school flag, literally a one-person team. Other schools had a flag bearer plus their athletics team marching behind it. Because I won so many events, Highfields State School received a place overall. My Dad was chuffed with that result and the story was told and retold many times. He was happy and there was peace at home.

In Grade 12, at Toowoomba State High School, I was offered a university scholarship to the United States for athletics. This was one of the 'sliding door' moments in my life; between staying an amateur or potentially becoming a professional athlete. I turned down the offer, a decision I did not regret. I needed to be at home, as the peace-makers were now only my little sister and me.

Competing in lane 2 for Toowoomba State High School. I managed to win and break a record despite the even start.

The following year, in 1986, I took a gap year prior to going to university to become a Physical Education (PE) teacher. My goal was to compete in the National Athletics Championships in the Heptathlon. The Heptathlon, a multi discipline contest, consists of seven events in which you compete over two days. I loved this event - the strategy and the focus it required. My childhood inspiration was Glennis Nunn, who had also gone to Toowoomba State High School. She had won the Heptathlon for Australia in the Brisbane Commonwealth Games in 1982. Glennis had then left her job as a PE teacher in 1983 to concentrate on training and won gold at the Los Angeles Olympic Games in 1984.

I remember my Dad hired a TV set that year for three months so we could watch Glennis compete. That was the first time we ever had television in the house. Whilst it was great to see what the hype about 'Neighbours' was, the TV was certainly the time waster Mum said it would be.

My parents had no spare money and there was little sponsorship available to me at the time, so I started working at KR Darling Downs meatworks, to support my athletics goal. I chose the meatworks as I could start work early, finish around two in the afternoon and do four or five hours training to cover the seven Heptathlon events. I also really liked salami, so I would put my hand up to work in the smallgoods section where I would happily smell processed meat all day long. Not everybody's cup of tea! My love of 'wurst' must have been my German heritage!

Soliciting a friend's help to fix my rusty old red Cortina

My first car was a rusty old red Cortina for which I paid $200. It broke down frequently and I had to rapidly learn how to troubleshoot and fix an alternator! I was tired of not having enough money. When a family friend suggested I join the Army, get a good salary and maybe even become a full-time athlete and compete for the Army, I asked, 'Where do I sign?' I knew I would be able to get a degree later, which I did.

I knew from my childhood that I did not want to be poor. Being poor had forced Mum and us to stay in a violent household. It limited her choices. Joining the Army seemed a logical step to take. Our friend did specify that I should join as a soldier first. Then if I wanted I could apply for

Royal Military College Duntroon and become an officer later. He believed that this experience would make me a better officer. That made sense to me. My upbringing, my athletics training, all ultimately led me to making my decision to join a disciplined organisation such as the Army. These traits would hold me in good stead to face one of the most gruelling and difficult courses the Army had to offer.

4 - JOINING THE ARMY

I have never regretted joining the Army. I have travelled the world, forged wonderful friendships and gained an abundance of skills and knowledge along the way. There have been many difficult and trying times throughout my Army career, but the good times have far outweighed the bad. I remain attached to the Army to this day. I joined up on 11th November, Armistice Day, 1986 aged 17. At the time I did not know that this was an historically significant date, as it was the day the peace agreement to end the First World War was signed. This meant I have never forgotten my enlistment date! I was leaving home, leaving my little sister looking after Mum - not what I wanted, but I needed to move on.

I was put on a bus at the Brisbane Army Recruiting Centre and sent to Kapooka - the 1st Recruit Training Unit based near Wagga Wagga in New South Wales - to do my basic training to become a soldier. Both men and women trained there and I was put in an all-women platoon.

The concept of female platoons was relatively new. Until December 1984, with the release of the Sex Discrimination Act 1985, women only attended Women's Royal Australian Army Corps (WRAAC) School at Georges Heights, Mosman in Sydney. A woman who had trained at the WRAAC School told me they used to carry shovels in place of rifles. This seemed unbelievable to me as we did the same training as the men with real rifles. Thankfully, we got paid the same too, but

I later worked with women who remembered when men were paid more. Until then, women were also required to discharge once they became pregnant. Fortunately, the Australian Defence Force (ADF) had progressed in that regard too. I was to learn later that it had not progressed in other areas in the employment of women, and was held back by archaic thinking male leaders not wanting change.

The Recruiting bus rolled to a stop beside a large looming dormitory. The singing and joviality of the last few hours ceased abruptly. All the girls and boys on the bus, with eyes like dinner plates, stared silently and anxiously as the door slid slowly open. A large impeccably dressed male soldier, with two stripes on his arm, burst onto the bus. I was to learn very soon that two stripes were the rank of Corporal. He was one of the Recruit Instructors who was going to rule our lives, 24 hours a day, for the next three months! He had a loud booming voice that nearly pierced my ear drums. And I thought Dad was a loud shouter! This Corporal yelled at us, quite impolitely, to 'Get off the fuckin' bus. NOW!' Of course, we obliged as rapidly as we could, tripping over each other in our haste. We hauled our heavy wheel-less suitcases and formed up beside the bus in a ragged semblance of order. The Corporal roared at us that we had formed up in a 'gaggle', which did not sound complimentary. We did not care. We all wished we were in a gaggle far, far away! Even though I was surrounded by chaos and one girl had started to cry, I still felt I was doing the right thing. This was day one of what would be a long and eventful career of service to my country. The change continued on the second day. My shoulder length hair was cut off, much to my horror. The Corporals had strongly suggested I would not have time to maintain it. They were right. It was one less thing to worry about, and I would grow it back!

*My first Army mug shot
- no words needed!*

My athletics training and my childhood work experiences held me in good stead. However, I soon learnt in the Army about the importance of teamwork and the team being as strong as its weakest member. Athletics is such an individual sport but I now enjoyed being part of a team, training as a team, learning the basic soldier skills that would turn me from Recruit Fellowes into Private Fellowes.

I do recall being called other names like Quarmbie, which I learnt refers to a highly uncoordinated person lacking in motor skills, usually on the drill square or when undertaking weapon handling. The sooner I fixed that mistake, the sooner the Corporal would stop calling me a Quarmbie. Unlike a number of girls in my platoon, I enjoyed the discipline, learning new skills like navigation, doing repetitious drills with our rifle, then doing them blindfolded, so we could rectify stoppages and strip and assemble our weapon at night.

Negotiating the climbing wall at Kapooka

I developed great friendships which have withstood the test of time. We suffered together, we learnt together and we grew into a team of trained soldiers. We learnt to trust one another and we knew we would always be there for one another, in good times and bad. It was fantastic to experience that mateship so young - one day we might rely on it for our lives! Even today, I always recommend family and friends to join the Military.

In some ways I was in the same position Mum had been when she came to Australia - I had left home at a young age, was now in a strange new environment, I was learning a new 'language' and being taught to think and act in a whole different way. My new 'sisters' were my platoon mates and we had to look out for one another, protect one another from getting into trouble and getting more punishment. For example, our shoes needed to be 'spit and polished' up to standard for the relentless inspections by our Instructors. I was never any good at this, so my roommates polished them for me. My contribution to my new sisterhood was helping them improve their running. During our Basic Fitness Test runs, I would run with the slower girls - those who were having trouble completing the run in the required time to pass. Nobody wanted to do the extra physical training if they failed. Life was already hard enough at Kapooka. So, I would run beside them, encouraging them to dig deep, go past the pain they were feeling, find that burst of energy to pass, even with a few seconds to spare!

At our Marching Out Parade, at the end of our basic training, I managed to win two out of the three awards presented - Best at Physical Training and Best Rifle Shot. It turns out that the school holidays I had spent being a jillaroo at Injune, western Queensland, had paid dividends. I had learnt to shoot by shooting kangaroos from the back of my boss's old Land Rover, whilst he drove wildly across the rough paddocks.

After the March Out Parade, I moved on to the next challenge, Initial Employment Training. This took another few months at the Army School of Ordnance, Bandiana, learning to become an Administration Clerk. We were a team now and we thought we could do anything. Well, except type, in my case. I had never used a typewriter before. To pass the course you had to type 35 words a minute. With extra training given to me by my course mates I managed to pass, just! I recall my Course Report saying: 'Robyn is easily distracted and then tends to disrupt the entire class.' So maybe my skill was my ability to influence, not my ability to type?

My first posting after my initial training was to Melbourne. This was my first job and I was keen to make a good impression. I said a sad goodbye to my platoon mates and we were catapulted in different directions around Australia. With my new name badge saying Private Fellowes, I landed in Melbourne, filled with nervous excitement. I would be posted to Central Army Records Office as a Staff Clerk. I would live here for at least two years according to my Posting Order. I had travelled around Australia competing in athletics, so was comfortable with different environments, but this time it was more permanent.

People from Melbourne were quite different from the laidback Queenslanders I was used to. For one thing they seemed to demonstrate almost zealot behaviour as they morphed into one-eyed crazy Australian Football League (AFL) fans on the weekends. They would be beeping their horns and have their club scarves and flags hanging out of their cars. Everybody seemed to know their club's song which would be sung loudly and repeatedly if their club was victorious. I thought I had better join them, so I chose to support the Saint Kilda team because that was where I was living. Choosing another team would not have been safe!

I also had to get used to driving with trams and doing box or hook turns, which is a right hand turn you make from the left-hand lane. Not intuitive at all, especially to a Queenslander. My first trip in a tram was just as dramatic. Firstly, the passengers in the tram thought my friend and I were tram conductors. We were dressed in our dark green military uniform, green striped blouse with a green cardigan and our 'duck hunting' hats, all designed by Prue Acton and universally despised. We were mumbling, 'No, we are in the Army', but the passengers did not believe us. 'Can I have a ticket?' they insisted. Then suddenly the tram lurched forward heading to the next stop. Unlike the other passengers, we did not know you had to hang on if you were standing. We both went crashing to the back of the tram landing in an untidy pile, hats going flying. Finally, dishevelled and wiser, we arrived at our first day of work. We definitely were not making the good impression we wanted, with uniforms and duck hunting hats covered in dirt and dust.

*In our infamous
'duck hunting hats'*

As one of the newest soldiers, I was immediately put on duty for my first weekend - a good way to get orientated, they said. The duty detail consisted of a Corporal and a Private for a 24-hour period and we were the Unit's point of contact for any incidents that occurred outside of work hours. The Corporal said she would show me the doors I needed to lock to secure the building. She handed me a large bunch of keys and headed into the lift, saying, 'Don't lose them. They are the master set.'

As I stepped into the lift behind her, the keys slipped through my nervous fingers and dropped through the gap between the floor and the lift. I helplessly watched as the keys disappeared into the darkness, crashing into the base of the lift shaft. All I could think was, 'Oh, no - I am in a lot of trouble now!' The Corporal turned around in the lift and looked at me where I had frozen in mid step with the blood drained from my face and replaced with a look of fear and disbelief. I had managed to lose the master set of keys in a matter of seconds! She looked at my empty hands and where I was pointing vigorously down the lift shaft and, shaking her head, said, 'No, surely you didn't.' I just nodded sheepishly. The Corporal walked back out the lift, not looking at me, and we walked silently back to the Duty Room to ring the 24hr Lift Support number. Phew! Although I was happy to hear from the lift technician that this was a common occurrence, the Corporal was not as impressed as she wrote up what had happened in the duty log. My incident meant I was suddenly well known in the Unit for being the first soldier to lose the set of master keys - reaching legendary status for all the wrong reasons. I also received another duty the following weekend, to ensure I had learnt from my mistake.

Despite my initial clumsiness I found myself in a positive environment where all levels of leadership looked after their subordinates. It was good solid leadership by men and by women. An experienced female Sergeant and Corporal both looked out for me. They were good role models. It was their positive influence that gave me the confidence to want to change and improve my situation by progressing up the ladder to achieve a higher rank. Perhaps I could become an officer one day.

In late 1987 my Unit was conducting individual military training in order to improve our recently acquired skills learnt at basic training. At this training we were fortunate to find ourselves being addressed by an experienced special forces soldier, a Warrant Officer. The subject was Guerrilla Warfare. The gruff Warrant Officer told us that guerrilla warfare was about covertly sending small elite trained, special forces teams into countries that required our assistance. Special forces were members of the military trained to conduct unconventional operations like guerrilla warfare or anti-terrorism. These teams would then engage with the country's local population. They would train these people, maybe arm them and assist them to conduct an operation or task. I found the concept very interesting and it made sense why the military would conduct these types of operations.

At the completion of his brief, I nervously put my hand up and asked the Warrant Officer if they had any women in these guerrilla warfare teams. I figured that would make sense, to have women in the team to engage with women in the society or community they were trying to influence. He looked at me bewildered and said gruffly, 'No, of course not!' I looked back at him equally bewildered, wondering how on earth they were able to effectively talk to and engage with the entire population. This enlightening and formative experience would shape many of my later decisions and actions.

After this training, I kept thinking about what that special forces Warrant Officer had said. If they only had men in the teams, surely they would only be engaging with half of the population - the other men. One thing I did know - men talk to men, women talk to women. You only have to look at an Australian barbecue as an example, where the men will group around the sizzling steaks and sausages with beer in hand talking and the women will gather in a separate group. I appreciated that gender roles are often based on common interests and cultural expectations. It seemed obvious to me you would need to have a mixed team, men and women, in order to successfully engage and conduct that type of covert mission. I realised that day that these differences were not taken into consideration on guerilla warfare operations.

That said, it would be later in my career, on my first tour overseas, that I would confirm, first hand, the importance of having men talk to men and women talk to women. The Army had commenced my training and although I didn't know it at the time, I would need everything that they had taught me…and much, much more…. to overcome the physical and mental challenges that lay ahead.

5 – CHANGING UP

It was a pivotal moment in my life when I decided I wanted to become an officer. I wanted to be able to make a difference. Yes, I now understood how to take orders and now I was ready to give orders. Although I had only experienced positive leadership, I humbly thought I could do a better job. After 18 months of soldiering, I applied to the Officer Selection Board whose role is to assess your leadership skills, motivation and commitment to duty and excellence.

I would describe myself as an introverted person, preferring to get on and get the job done - quietly influencing people to achieve an outcome. This approach, however, would not get me noticed at the Officer Selection Board. I had to be assertive and outgoing to be noticed by the board members. I would have to do impromptu public speaking on an 'off the cuff' subject. My worst nightmare, public speaking! So, I addressed this weakness by practising speaking in front of my friends on topics they chose. Working outside my personal comfort zone was the norm in 'this man's army'. I was relieved when I passed the selection board. My parents were very pleased. Dad would proudly say, 'Rank has its privileges.' Clearly Dad had thought he outranked all of us!

Years later I would become a Selection Board member and I always looked out for the introverted candidate, the one who had the ability and potential if you looked past the shyness. It was the mission of the Royal Military College, Duntroon in

Canberra, to develop the selected candidates into future leaders. The college promotes leadership, integrity and the pursuit of excellence. I was to learn the difference between being a leader and being a manager. You lead people and you manage resources. The college would teach us both.

Having passed the officer selection course in 1988, I headed to Canberra to commence training to become an Officer in the Australian Army. I was fit, I was focused and knew instinctively I was taking the next correct step in my career. I was no longer Private Fellowes; I was now Staff Cadet Fellowes.

An impeccably dressed Staff Cadet Fellowes

As a Staff Cadet, and a member of the Corps of Staff Cadets, you are allocated to one of the five companies. I was allocated to Gallipoli Company and our company mascot was the Michelin Man. This depicted the tough and hardy tyres that would not puncture easily. We quickly imbued that same toughness into our officer training.

During the course we progressed from Third Class to Second Class to First Class over an 18-month period. In Third Class, we started with 12 female cadets. 18 months later only two of us graduated. I thought this was an appalling statistic. Most of the women who did not graduate either chose to leave because they were being given a hard time by the male cadets or were discharged due to physical injuries from the arduous military training.

This was after the historic 1983 scandal at Duntroon took place, involving the abusive behaviours called 'bastardisation' - the abuse of institutional powers by means of inappropriate discipline and punishment. However, it appeared nothing had improved in terms of a change of culture and the acceptance of women. I witnessed my fellow female cadets receiving additional pressure from the male cadets because of their injuries. Women were certainly treated worse. We were called Squids, Sluts, Dykes. I was none of those things and I objected to how we were treated. I asked the Head Cadet, a Senior Under Officer, to stand up for the women, in particular the injured women. We deserved to be treated the same as the men. We deserved a fair go. Duntroon is hard enough without receiving additional unfair peer pressure! I do not recall seeing the male cadets applying the same pressure to other injured male cadets. The Senior Under Officer said he would not intervene. What? I was disgusted! What a poor demonstration of leadership - not the style of leadership we were there to learn. I thought we were learning to do the right thing. However, just because everybody is doing it does not make it right. Just because you are the only person doing something, does not make it wrong! Then my worst nightmare occurred… I was injured too!

I broke my ankle playing netball whilst in Second Class. I was pushed over by a more senior cadet whilst going for a goal, and came down on the side of my ankle. I heard the crack as I came crashing down. Lying on the netball court grasping my ankle I felt at the lowest point of my short career. The medical staff said it was just a bad sprain, and I would be fine in a week, but I was not.

Although I kept going for the next three months, doing all the challenging physical activities, I knew something was very wrong. I asked for an x-ray and it proved my ankle was broken. I knew if the injury was severe enough and the pressure great enough, I could be back squadded - which is sent back to the previous class - or removed from Duntroon. In the worst case, I could have been medically discharged from the Army.

I was determined to stay in my class if I possibly could. Having just done three months of this arduous course with an undiagnosed broken ankle, I believed I had earned the right to stay. I asked permission from the Instructing Staff to remain in the same class. I told them I would provide them with a Gold Pass - the highest-level pass you could achieve on our Basic Fitness Test (a 2.4 km run in a blistering time and a punishing number of pushups and situps) - if they let me stay. I was elated when they accepted. I knew I had a lot of rehabilitation work to do on top of completing the already packed academic schedule.

Fortunately our class had a short leave break and I was able to spend this time at home being looked after by Mum.

I still deployed on all the military activities over the next six weeks and I found myself sitting on the safety radio network. I did not mind being on the radio due to my ankle injury, although I would have preferred to be out in the bush with my fellow cadets. During the survival exercise there were no rations provided, but each group was given a live chicken in a cage. One group had been unable to bring themselves to kill it. If I had been in that group that chook would have been killed, plucked and cooked without a second thought. Mum had taught us all to do this back on the farm.

Back in Duntroon after our leave, I was on my crutches, doing my best to keep up behind 120 cadets marching briskly along as we went from lecture to lecture. This required me to quickly become very proficient on crutches. I relied heavily on my knowledge as an athlete to rehabilitate my ankle, as well as the proficient medical staff, to honour my word of a Gold Pass. I proudly completed my Gold Pass and moved into First Class, the final six months before graduation.

One of the military activities we all had to do in First Class was a Parachute Water Jump into Jervis Bay. It was supposed to be a low risk activity designed to show us one method of entry into the battlefield. We received our training for the static line jump at the navy base HMAS Albatross and boarded the C130 Hercules aircraft. This was my first time in a military aircraft. To say that I felt apprehensive would be a serious understatement.

Once over the drop zone, Jervis Bay, the back door of the C130 opened up like a huge yawning mouth, unfortunately showing us how high we were. The Senior Instructor, who was also a qualified paratrooper, stood near the opening bellowing at us over the engine noise, 'So who wants to go first?' I was trying to hide behind the cadet in front of me. I did not like heights and I certainly did not want to jump out of this perfectly good aircraft first! 'Hey, Fellowes, you look like you want to go first. Come up here and I will hook you on,' he yelled with a wicked smile on his face.

Suddenly there I was, standing beside him, hooked on. 'OK, off you go,' and with a helpful push I was gone. The parachute opened with a scary jerk and I was sailing quickly down into Jervis Bay. What they had omitted to tell us during our training was that Jervis Bay was a breeding ground for hammerhead sharks! I was getting close to the water now and my parachute and I were heading straight for the largest hammerhead shark I had ever seen. The closer I got, the bigger it got!

I had developed a fear of sharks as a child swimming past the breakers at Sunrise Beach in Noosa. I was swimming underwater one day, when I saw a large shark out of the corner of my eye swimming parallel with the beach. I froze. The only things that were moving were my hands to keep myself under the water, in the same position. My wide terrified eyes watched this shark as it swam nonchalantly in front me, a couple of metres away. It was at least three times as big as me! As soon as it disappeared into the bluish gloom, I came straight up out the water and swam as fast as I could towards shore, imagining the shark was right behind me. Thankfully I caught the first wave in. I think if I had panicked, surfaced and swum for the shore when I first saw it, the outcome may not have been so good. Although I was a strong swimmer, I was just a kid and there was no way I could have outswum that enormous shark.

Now I was potentially going to land on one! I knew that this huge hammerhead shark would not be happy being startled like that! I started to pull on the toggle ropes trying to steer my parachute into the safety boat near the shark – not what we were supposed to do. I almost succeeded, but the instructor in the boat saw what was happening and quickly gunned the engine. He moved the boat so I landed in the water right beside it instead. Bugger! I hit the water then came straight back up and launched myself over the side of the safety boat. The Instructor put his hand on my head and pushed me back in the water, 'You know the drill, parachute first.' 'But there is a bloody great big shark just there,' I yelled at him. 'Nope, parachute first,' he said, unconcerned. I bundled up my parachute in record speed and heaved it at him. Then without any assistance I launched myself back into the boat. I had just been forced to deal with two of my greatest fears - heights and sharks! I lay on the floor of the boat, soaking wet, relieved and above all, safe, as I watched my classmates start to hit the water around me.

In 1989 I graduated from Duntroon. I was proud of my achievement and ready to leave that officer training environment behind. My parents came down to Canberra for my graduation, and Dad was on his best behaviour - proud of my accomplishment, just like in the old athletics days.

I was commissioned as a Lieutenant, and was allocated to the Royal Australian Corps of Signals (RA Sigs). The primary role of RA Sigs is the provision of military communications.

I was at the bottom of the officer pile, and spent the next two years in Signals Corps units. We trained on exercises and operations to provide the seamless communications essential to manoeuvring troops and directing units on the battlefield. Signals Corps was a combat-related Corps and not all combat-related Corps were open to women at that time. Again, a situation that did not make sense to me. I had become an officer so I could make a difference. Maybe I would get an opportunity to address this inequity down the track.

Learning to become a Signals Corps officer

6 – TIME TO STEP UP

At the age of 22 I found myself in my third year as a Lieutenant and soon to be commanding a platoon of 30 female recruits. It was not where I wanted to be, but perhaps I needed to be here. I would be required to make the right decisions and make critical changes to protect my platoon, even if not supported by the leadership.

My Career Advisor was trying to sell me the idea of a posting back to Kapooka, saying we needed our best officers training recruits. The trouble was I did not want to go to Kapooka at that time. I wanted to go to Cambodia. My Signals Unit had been mobilised to go to Cambodia on a United Nations (UN) peacekeeping mission. We were all so excited! Well, I was, until I saw my posting order to Wagga Wagga! Deflated and upset, I was told that another officer would deploy with my troop to Cambodia in my place.

With a brave smile I waved my colleagues off and trudged back to Kapooka. I had also waved goodbye to the love of my life, as he was sent to Cambodia too. I said I would wait for him, but he told me not to wait. I had wanted to get married and have kids. He did not. I was heartbroken. I never saw him again as our lives went in different directions. Although the military life gave me many other opportunities to form meaningful relationships, none was like that first one. In those days it was harder for a woman to combine a military career with a family life.

Back at Kapooka, not overly happy

My unwanted return to Kapooka was in the role of a Platoon Instructor. I was in command of a platoon as it undertook the three-month recruiting course - the one I had undertaken a few short years before. I knew the course was physically and mentally challenging as it turned civilians into soldiers. Our role as Instructors was not only to instruct but also to be a positive role model to the recruits. I remembered having very good role models when I did my recruit training and so I knew I could be a good role model too.

This was a platoon of scared, wide-eyed female recruits. It was a look and a feeling I could certainly empathise with! My reason for being back there quickly became apparent when I saw the high number of female recruits in other platoons suffering from fractured pelvises. I knew from my experience as an athlete that men and women are physiologically different. I knew that a woman has a larger and broader pelvis for childbirth, whereas a man has a narrower, more compact, stronger pelvis. That was clear in the gender differences in National and World records in most sports. This was my opportunity to immediately put in place strategies to prevent such injuries occurring in my platoons.

This meant going against the training policy of the day, so I did this surreptitiously. It was the first of many times in my military career I thought it better to seek forgiveness than permission. This approach allowed me to do the right thing even if it was not in accordance with current policy. It had also earnt me the nickname Teflon Fellowes, sometimes doing the right thing, but sometimes bending the rules and getting away with it. In this instance, I would get my female recruits to remove their packs when they were going to be jumping from a height which could cause them pelvic injury. They were still able to achieve the task, but in a way that nobody got hurt.

At my Platoon's March Out Parade, talking with my Officer Commanding

Those women who were injured in other platoons, who suffered serious fractured pelvic injuries, were medically discharged from the Army. These women would potentially have serious issues later in life with childbirth, and certainly chronic pain. This made me angry and frustrated because it was so easily avoided! I was not going to allow something so preventable to happen to one of my recruits. Men and women are built differently for a reason, so we should work with our differences, not pretend we are the same. Our differences are our strength! I was able to make the right decision and protect these young women from serious injury.

7 – WOMEN TALK TO WOMEN

My first tour overseas was my first real exposure to the gendered nature of the human environment on the international stage. It was here that I first understood how the differences between men and women were not being fully considered by the military on this mission. Not only did this result in sexual and gender-based violence against women and girls being ignored - these women were also isolated from being involved in the peace process. I was to learn that this was a clear warning sign that this region was likely to struggle to find enduring peace in the future.

In 1998, at the rank of Captain, I finally received my first Deployment Order to go overseas. This was on Operation Bel-Isi, in Bougainville, as a Patrol Commander in the Defence Peace Monitoring Group. I was incredibly excited to be going - especially after my disappointment of not going to Cambodia. My home for the next five months was to be Bougainville, an automonous region of Papua New Guinea (PNG). Bougainville is the largest island in the Solomon Islands archipelago to the north east of Australia, some 2397 kilometres from Brisbane. The island is predominantly a tropical rain forest, with many rivers and mountains which make movement challenging.

The conflict was between the Bougainville Revolutionary Army (BRA) and the PNG Defence Force. The rebellion ran for nearly ten years, sparked by land ownership issues with the Panguna Mine, an Australian run gold and copper mine. Nearly 20,000 people died. It was a disaster on our doorstep and it required a regional response. The Peace Monitoring Group consisted of troops from Fiji, Vanuatu, Tonga, New Zealand, Australia and Solomon Islands. Our role was to assist in developing an awareness of the Ceasefire Agreement signed in Arawa Township on 30 April 1998. It was a regional peacekeeping operation and although we were not armed, I heard there were caches of weapons on the island.

As part of my officer professional development I had embarked on studying a Human Resources degree externally. I thought this deployment would be a good opportunity to do some research and obtain original data for my next assignment: *Change within a Society or Organisation*. Through my initial research, I discovered Bougainville was primarily a matrilineal society and customary land ownership was generally traced through maternal lineage. I also knew the conflict was caused by land ownership issues associated with the Panguna Mine. I was looking forward to interviewing local Bougainvilleans and gathering some data. I would look at three phases, pre-conflict, conflict and post conflict, from their perspective.

I was more than ready. This was my first deployment, my first time on a Navy ship, HMAS TOBRUK, to reach Bougainville. I loved the experience of being on a ship. I was impressed how well the Navy ship's crew worked together. I guess they had to. If there was a fire on the ship, they would all go down! I paid special attention to the safety briefs. The sea sickness tablets I was taking every day made me sleepy. I now knew I had joined the Army, not the Navy, for a reason! I would hear the sirens going off for another practice fire alert. Fortunately, I was not required to respond to this drill, just the navy crew. I would roll over in my bunk and go back to sleep, content to go down with the ship. I would not wake until the next morning when the Officer of the Day would boom over the internal sound system, 'Wakey, wakey, hands off snakey!' - not relevant to those few women on board, but it made me chuckle.

We arrived in Bougainville in mid-April 1998. As we finished disembarking HMAS TOBRUK, we stood on the dock and watched the Bougainville Peace Delegation embark so they could conduct high level peace talks. The ship provided an excellent venue for the talks as suitable meeting rooms were not available in Bougainville. As I watched, I was surprised to see no women in the peace delegation. This did not make sense to me, as I expected women to be a substantial part of the peace delegation due to their role in this primary matrilineal society. I would need to check that out later.

Speaking Tok Pisin (known as Pidgin English), the common language spoken in Bougainville, was very important in order to engage with the population. Our contingent had studied Tok Pisin and other cultural and military aspects on the eight-day voyage to Bougainville. We also undertook mine and explosive ordnance training to prepare ourselves for the deployment. I kept studying Tok Pisin throughout my tour, believing it was critical that we were able to speak the local dialect, even if not fluently. I was in their country so I should do my best to speak their language. My patrol's mission was to go into different villages within our assigned Area of Operations, to engage with the local population on the peace process. I would address the ceasefire awareness meetings in Tok Pisin as part of my role as a Patrol Commander.

At one of the ceasefire awareness meetings I introduced myself in my best Tok Pisin, and explained our role. Suddenly, there was a thunderclap overhead announcing a storm. After years of warfare, the seasoned locals immediately threw themselves to the ground for cover, fearing an incoming mortar round. Then a novice field soldier, I remained standing at the microphone, only thinking it could be thunder. It was a surreal moment as I looked around me wondering if it was wise to be the only person standing if another bolt of lightning was imminent. Years later, after experiencing constant rocket and missile fire in Middle East, I no longer stood in the face of danger just like these war weary Bougainville locals, never assuming it was only thunder. Back then I still had a lot to learn in this job!

I discovered within weeks of being in Bougainville that it was actually a patriarchal society in application. All the leaders, chiefs and heads of villages were male. Because of this I would let my Second-in-Command (2IC), a male Fijian Lieutenant, talk to the male village chiefs, while I, as the only female in the patrol, would speak to the women from the village. I already knew men talk to men and women talk to women, so I thought I would get slightly different

Myself, a team member and my 2IC, George, taking a break and having a refreshing coconut drink

information. I just did not know how different! The chiefs would say they were happy with the peace process, the situation was calm and everything was progressing well. The women I spoke to told me the opposite. They told me they and their children were being threatened and harmed by armed gangs of youths. They were being raped and their daughters were being raped. They had no freedom of movement and as a result, they were not involved in the peace process.

Wherever we went, I would get the same story from the women. They spoke openly and freely to me, as another woman. I had verified the fraught security situation for the women and girls and now understood why I did not see any women in the peace delegation a few weeks earlier. I thought,

'We have a safety and security situation here.' Now that I had identified the problem, I asked the women what I could do to help them - what were the solutions to their concerns. They said they needed to be able to get together with other women in the area so they could discuss the security situation and the peace process. They badly needed my help because moving safely around the island since the start of the conflict was virtually impossible.

I briefed my Commanding Officer on the security problem in our area and asked if I could assist the women as they had requested. My Commander said, 'No, you can't, as it is not part of the mission.' Seriously? I understood our role as the Peace Monitoring Group was to facilitate the ceasefire agreement. But surely if 50% of the population, and their concerns, were being excluded, it would be difficult for that peace process to proceed successfully. So, based on my assessment, surely it **was** our problem. I was glad I persisted, as he finally relented and said I could help the women, but I could only work on the task during my time off!

I happily used my limited time off to write formal military messages to our Headquarters in Arawa requesting additional resources in the form of vehicles, boats and helicopters. We needed all these forms of transport to bring these women together for a forum. We ended up with over 300 willing female participants from across the country at our team site in Tonu. The women discussed how they could improve the appalling security situation for themselves and their children, the most vulnerable. They talked about how these security concerns could be factored into the peace process. The women exchanged ideas for several days. Sitting back listening to the women talk, sometimes with the help of an interpreter when they spoke too fast, I realised we had learnt a lot from this small task.

I had learnt that we should assist all those who needed a helping hand - the vulnerable people. This would add value to the achievement of our mission. However, I felt that we had deployed into this mission without a deliberate plan to engage with the entire population on the peace process, only the male leaders and chiefs. It would take many years for this failure or omission in planning processes to change. It was primarily because I was doing research for my university assignment, and after gaining a deeper understanding of the situation, that I began to engage directly with the women. I heard many years later that a position had been created in the Peace Monitoring Group Headquarters that focussed on engaging with women. Definitely a much-needed change.

I wrote my university assignment on my return to Australia and I changed the focus of my paper, due to my experience, to how **women** had been affected by the conflict in Bougainville. I was to find out many years later that United Nations Security Council Resolution 1325 (UNSCR 1325), Women, Peace and Security, signed off in 2000, was created because of these very reasons. The Security Council Resolution formally acknowledged the changing nature of warfare in which civilians are increasingly targeted and women and girls are disproportionately affected by conflict.

Negotiating a river on the way to the village peace meeting

Spending time with the girls and boys in the village

After conflict, women were then being excluded from participation in peace processes. The resolution specifically addressed how women and girls are differently impacted by conflict, and recognised the critical role that women have in peace making and peace building efforts.

Several months into my time in Bougainville, I experienced the same fear the Bougainville women had spoken to me about. I had briefed my Commander that it was too dangerous to be conducting our peace monitoring engagements without a vehicle, due to the worsening security situation. Our team had damaged a vehicle in a failed river crossing, so we only had one vehicle. My boss, however, still wanted us to continue with our meetings. I nominated myself and two patrol members to be dropped off by our only vehicle. We would walk into the village and conduct the meeting. The other half of my patrol would drive to the next village and conduct their meeting. At the conclusion of our meetings, the plan was to meet at a rendezvous point and drive back to the team site together. The first village was a considerable hike, so I selected the two fittest male members to come with me.

We completed the meeting and were heading back to the rendezvous point when we came around a bend and the road was blocked by about 50 machete-wielding youths. 'Oh shit!' My first thought was I would be lucky if I was just killed. I immediately tucked my long blonde plait into my hat, pulled my hat down over my hair and face, and tucked myself in close between the tall, lanky Special Forces soldier and the male Foreign Affairs civilian on my other side. Both of them were talking to the youths, being very friendly, talking loudly and joking with the menacing youths as we approached. We had to pause as the youths slowly and reluctantly parted so we could move though, their ranks closing immediately behind us. I kept my gaze on the ground, and didn't utter a single word. I did not want to draw attention to myself. Being tall, blonde and female, it was not that easy. I was trying to look as small and uninteresting as possible. We were followed by the group for what seemed like an eternity. My two 'bodyguards' continued the banter - saying 'goodbye' many, many times as we kept walking briskly with our large posse of aggressive youths right behind us.

Finally, they stopped following us. There was immense relief from all of us. We broke into a run and sprinted the rest of the way to the vehicle pickup point in case they changed their minds. As we jumped into the back of the vehicle I thanked my two bodyguards for keeping their cool. The soldier said, 'Ma'am you did the right thing. We all did the right thing.' He was right, we had. If any of us had done anything different the outcome may have not been so good.

I was annoyed that my Commander had not listened to me and I was put in that position. That evening, as I wrote up my patrol report, I recommended that foot patrols in that area should not occur again until the security situation improved. Foot patrols were too vulnerable and only vehicle patrols should be used. I knew our patrol had a close call and I did not want it to happen to someone else - man or woman!

Shortly after the incident, a military psychologist was visiting our team site talking with all of us in turn. I told the story about the incident with the aggressive group of armed youths quite matter-of-factly. The psychologist, however, picked up something in my voice and asked me a few more questions. I realised then that at the time I had feared for my life, of being raped, killed or both. I had felt extremely vulnerable - a vulnerability unlike I had ever felt before. We were unarmed and at the mercy of those armed youths. I knew from my discussions with the women in villages what these youths were capable of doing. I realised that I had never known that fear before - the fear the Bougainville women and girls faced every day. On one hand I felt so fortunate that I was born a female in Australia, but on the other hand I realised how important it was for us to help those women and girls. I felt much better after the chat with the psychologist. I made sure my soldiers learnt the importance of being debriefed by a psychologist even if they felt they had nothing to say.

I believe it was important for this peacekeeping mission that we were unarmed. The benefits certainly outweighed the risks. The Peace Monitoring Group was able to successfully monitor the ceasefire agreement and the Bougainvilleans were able to broker an agreement. They regained control of their public service, courts, police, correctional institutions, taxation and foreign aid initiatives. Women have contributed to the post-conflict restoration for the past two decades, and are members of the Autonomous Bougainville Government. The peace has continued, as has Bougainville's desire to become an independent country. Unfortunately, I expect this will be a future flash point in the South West Pacific.

The release of UN Security Council Resolution 1325 (UNSCR 1325) 'Women Peace and Security' now ensures that member nations, like Australia, engage with women from the start of missions similar to that in Bougainville. I did not know at the time that I was already implementing these principles and my understanding of them would shape my actions for the rest of my career.

8 - GOING COMMANDO

The term 'going commando' is a military colloquialism meaning wearing no underwear. However, I did not participate in this practice - rather the title of this chapter refers to another momentous and life-changing occurrence during my Army career.

As I progressed through my career I found myself increasingly looking through a gender lens. I began to understand how critical it was to have a military force that had the ability to engage with both men and women in the communities we encountered. There was no 'front line' on the battlefield any more. We needed to ensure men and women were trained the same so we could operate effectively anywhere, even behind enemy lines.

In the latter part of 1998, I was relaxing on a Friday afternoon after work, having a beer at the bar in an Officers' Mess in Sydney. I was approached by a special forces officer, who later went on to become the Commander of Special Forces. He asked if I wanted to participate in the trial of women conducting the Commando Selection course. I could not believe what I was hearing! I remembered back ten years ago when the special forces Warrant Officer could not understand why women would do guerrilla warfare roles. I could not understand why they would **not** – and now I was being given an opportunity to prove what I had always believed, that women could fulfil these roles, alongside the men. I was more than excited! What an amazing moment! But I did not want to sound too keen. I pretended to carefully consider his offer, and finally said, 'Yes, I could do that. Thank you for thinking of me.' He had worked with me the year before and I had a lot of respect for him. I was elated that I was being given an opportunity to prove that women could pass a special forces selection course.

I had learnt in Bougainville that having women as part of your military force was critical in engaging with the entire community, not just the male half. This was the opportunity I had been waiting for and I felt if anyone could pass a special forces course, it would be me. Not that I was special, but I knew I was physically and mentally resilient and determined to succeed, a result of my childhood - the domestic violence, working very hard from a young age - and my athletics career. These things taught me discipline and focus. I knew men who were Commandos and men who were in the Special Air Service Regiment. Each of them had struck me as a calm, capable and humble person - the type of person I was. I was trainable because I was not arrogant - I was curious and willing to learn. I knew exactly why I needed to pass this course. I had a point to prove. Women **were** capable of conducting the Commando Selection course.

I knew Commandos were amphibious raiding units which operate against strategic targets, normally using covert entry to achieve surprise. I knew the Commando Selection course was specifically designed to put candidates under duress, both physically and mentally, to see if they had the suitable attributes to be an effective Commando. The selection course tested your psychological resolve - your ability to problem solve whilst physically and mentally fatigued and undergoing sleep and food deprivation. I wanted to prove that women had the same capacity for physical and mental toughness as men - that they could be trained to an exceptional high level, and perform as expected. Women were serving in special forces units doing support roles. However, the Army did not have any women who had qualified to wear a special forces beret in either the Commandos or the Special Air Service Regiment. It was time for this to change.

I was given a three-month training schedule to prepare me for the initial barrier test. I would have to pass this test on the first day of the actual selection course to allow me to undertake the course. This initial test consisted of a timed 3km run with rifle and patrol order (basic equipment worn whilst patrolling), followed by a run, dodge and jump course and a climb up and down the ropes twice. I knew physiologically as a female I had less upper body strength than males and I had a lower centre of balance. This simplistically means that generally men can do a lot of push ups and women can do a lot of sit-ups. So, in my training I did everything they told me plus I did extra work to improve my upper body strength. I did chin ups and push ups and extra time in the gym.

I was doing this preliminary training schedule, while posted at Middle Head in Sydney, as one of the Operations Staff in a busy Headquarters with a high tempo. We were working long days. I would therefore have to train at nights and on weekends to fit in the 'full on' training. I hit the walking trails around Mosman in full battle kit, working up to the 20km marches our training schedule demanded. I was also getting my feet used to wearing my boots for these long marches, knowing we would march much further on the course, under more arduous physical and mental conditions.

During these training marches I would carry a steel pipe with a handle, weighing the same as our current service rifle, to simulate the real rifle we would carry on the selection course. I did not want to scare the locals. So, as I met people out for a walk on the trails, I would say a loud friendly 'Hello' well in advance. I did not want them to think I was a crazy military nut armed with a steel pipe, and call the police! That said, I did not realise I would soon need this pipe to save myself from attack.

Early one Sunday morning I was completing a 20km walk in full battle kit, including backpack, walking through a park in Mosman. I was nearly finished - sore and tired from head to foot. I could not wait to take my boots off. Suddenly, out of nowhere, this huge Doberman rushed at me, teeth bared and growling ferociously. Having grown up with dogs on a farm, I knew instinctively that this one was trouble. Unfortunately, I must have looked like a threat to this dog, which I could understand, given how I was dressed. My flight or fight response was yelling 'flight.' However, I could not move fast in my heavy 'battle rattle'. My legs were starting to seize up from the last 20km march. I used my steel 'rifle' to keep the snarling beast at bay as I backed away. As I was yelling for it to 'Piss off!' I knew this dog hadn't been called 'Pissoff'. It was probably called

'Brutus' or 'Crusher'! So, we danced - 'Brutus' remaining just out of range of my 'rifle' and me turning as it kept circling me, looking for a chance to rush in. I kept thinking, 'Where the hell is Brutus's owner?' I didn't dare take my eyes off the Doberman to look around.

After what seemed like an eternity, I heard the dog's owner yelling for it to 'Come back', which thankfully it did. I stood still, and only lowered my 'rifle' when the dog was put into an expensive Audi. As much as I wanted to go over and give the dog's owner a piece of my mind about letting vicious dogs off their leads in a public park, I thought it might backfire if he released the dog on me again. I dragged myself home as quickly as my exhausted, cramped legs would allow, mumbling under my breath about posh 'Mosmanites' being irresponsible dog owners. Later on, I thought I would have been very unlucky to have done all this training and then ended up in hospital from a dog attack! I chuckled. I had dodged a bullet - or dodged a dog. Or had I?

Two days before the start of the Commando Selection course I was doing my final run through the streets of Mosman late in the evening. It was pouring rain, it was dark and suddenly I felt shooting pain in my ankle, as it twisted and I fell heavily onto the wet bitumen road. I had rolled my ankle in a pot hole that I could not see in the darkness and rain. I raised my head from the bitumen to see a car racing towards me on the road, its headlights glaring through the heavy rain. I desperately rolled off the road into the gutter. It was probably that Audi-driving Doberman owner, who uncaringly sailed past splashing my already sodden clothes again! I dragged myself up so I was sitting on the gutter, with my feet being drenched by the fast-flowing ice-cold water. I was crying tears of pain and frustration. That ankle had never been the same since I broke it during my officer training at Duntroon. It was my 'Achilles heel'. The timing of this was devastating. How on earth was I going to start one of the most challenging selection courses in the Australian military in 48 hours? I could not even stand up!

It was a long slow hobble home, with my ankle barely able to take my body weight. I felt and looked like an old woman hobbling along in dire need of a walking stick or crutches, or both. I finally made it home. Even though I just wanted to curl up in a ball and cry tears of self-pity, I knew I had to improve this ankle as soon as possible. I rested it, iced it, bandaged it and elevated it. As an athlete, I had always had good results with acupuncture for rapid healing. So early the next morning I rang a local acupuncturist. I was desperate. 'You have to see me,' I said. 'I have 36 hours for you to fix my ankle. I need it to perform at its best! If you help me I will sing like a bird. I will tell all my army mates what you did.' I think my desperate pleas swayed him and we managed to fit in two needling appointments. Then, with a very tightly strapped ankle, full of trepidation, I turned up to do the initial barrier test at Randwick Barracks.

I was very aware you had to be at peak fitness before you start this course, and the large group of young motivated people I observed were bristling with fitness. I walked slowly up to the start of the 3km run in my patrol order complete with weapon. I prayed my ankle would just 'keep it together' so I could get through this test. I passed the 3km run and went immediately into the run, dodge and jump course, focussing on not rolling my ankle. When I got to the ropes, my extra upper body training paid off. I was just happy to do an activity that put no weight on my ankle. I did not want to come down the rope. Done! I had passed. We had barely caught our breath when the successful candidates were bundled onto buses and driven somewhere in the Blue Mountains to start the actual Commando Selection course. It was winter and the only thing that was hot was my inflamed ankle. There were two other women who had passed the test. I knew one. Lieutenant Deb Warren-Smith was a very competent, smart and capable intelligence corps officer. If she qualified she would be a great asset to the Army - a commando intelligence officer, and a woman!

 The course was as arduous and as gruelling as it had promised to be - constantly doing activities and tasks while deprived of food and sleep. The situation was constantly changing, testing every candidate's psychological resolve. It was bitterly cold in the Blue Mountains and I saw firsthand how the onset of hypothermia affects people's ability to function and make decisions. I saw the Medics step in only when the candidates could no longer safely conduct the activity. The safety vehicles would turn up and take those candidates away for medical attention. Often the candidate would not be allowed to return to the course. To my horror, I once witnessed the entire sole of a young man's foot come off in one piece during a 30km march. His foot was red raw. I could not imagine how he could even put his weight on it. But he was bandaged up and he bravely kept marching. Amazing resilience!

During that 30km march we were met with a never-ending flow of wicked problems to solve. The challenges were designed to wear us down, to test our leadership and teamwork, to demonstrate if we displayed the required attributes. I saw one candidate 'snap' when he thought we had reached our objective with our very heavy sand filled 'injured pilot' that we had been lugging on a stretcher. We were to hand over the pilot at this point and take a much-needed break. The Instructor then informed us that the 'safe' rendezvous point had been compromised by the enemy and now we had to keep on going. That candidate disappeared at that point, and did not reappear. Becoming angry when things go wrong was not one of the attributes the Instructors were looking for. Candidate numbers kept dropping daily.

This was the first time women had been on a special forces selection course, so there were media people roaming around. I kept as low a profile as possible and firmly maintained that I did not want to be interviewed. This whole process of allowing publicity seemed counter-intuitive to conducting covert operations in the future.

As the course continued - food and sleep deprivation, and the requirement to be able to think, give orders, listen to orders, conduct difficult and challenging tasks - I felt I was really coming into my own. The harder it got, the calmer I got!

As the physical and mental duress continued, I calmly watched as these super-fit human beings seemed to come down to the same level as me with my injured ankle. I had the offending ankle re-strapped on day three and then just got on with it - this was not the time to demonstrate any weakness.

Then it was my turn to be the patrol leader. I had to conduct a reconnaissance and then plan and execute a night raid to rescue a 'scientist' who had been kidnapped by the enemy. At one point, we had to climb up a narrow wire rope ladder to scale a steep rocky wall. This ensured our covert approach to the enemy position where our kidnap victim was located. All these tasks were more difficult when done at night and we were extremely mentally and physically fatigued. I remember my ankle not enjoying the highly unstable climb up the skinny ladder rungs. Not being a fan of heights, I was happy it was dark. My whole team performed well. We successfully executed the raid, killed the enemy and handed our scientist over to friendly forces, our Instructors.

One of the Instructors tapped me on the shoulder and said, 'Get to the back, Fellowes, you're Tail End Charlie now.' I knew what that meant. I had finished the final leadership test. One of my course mates would now be patrol leader. Tag, you're it! I felt so good! I would have had a grin from ear to ear had my muscles been capable of so much movement.

I gratefully moved to the rear of our patrol, nodding and whispering encouragement to my team mates as I went. My role at the rear of the patrol was to make sure we were not followed up by the enemy. We did another raid and headed back to the safe rendezvous point - the course almost over. I followed up the patrol, walking along the edge of a road, checking behind me occasionally. As we patrolled alongside the road, I was convinced I saw a line of large pink elephants walking in the opposite direction on the other side of the road. It was a small herd, about six of them. They all were linked, the trunk of the one behind holding the tail of the one in front, as they lumbered along, gently swaying from side to side. It was very calming watching each huge but peaceful pink elephant pass me by. I could feel the fatigue draining from my body. Once the last elephant passed me, I had a calm peaceful expression on my face. I was ready for the next raid! I checked behind to see if the elephants had turned around and were following us up. They had disappeared. 'Hmmm! That was weird, but nice!' I thought.

Several years later, when I was receiving a lesson from a very experienced special forces officer, he told us of his experience when trying to climb Mount Everest. He had to turn around, just before the summit because he was running out of oxygen. As he headed back down the mountain, heading for safety, he saw a line of pink elephants walking beside him, linked just as mine had been. I figured the pink elephant mirage must be a calming thing the mind does when a person is so incredibly fatigued. It takes you to a happy place and reinvigorates you.

The selection course taught me that my mind was much stronger than my body. I had started one of the most challenging and arduous courses in the Army with a serious ankle injury. This course is usually only attempted by people who are at their peak of physical fitness. I had passed the course purely because my mind **was** stronger than my body. The relentless stream of challenges had reduced us all to the same level. Then it was up to each of us to demonstrate the physical and mental resolve, the toughness, the teamwork and the leadership they were after. Many of the young, fit, capable and competent young men had failed, but the other two women and I had passed. A 100% success rate for the women! None of the male candidates who passed with us seemed surprised. You are selected because you meet the course requirements and are deemed to have the qualities they want in a Commando.

I felt immensely relieved to have passed this course, and was looking forward to the next challenge - to pass the suite of commando courses to qualify for the Green Beret. These included how to conduct advanced close quarter battle and urban fighting techniques; how to enter the battlefield via parachute; how to operate tactical small boats on amphibious operations, and many more skills needed by a member of a commando team.

We had proved that women were capable of achieving the same qualification as the men. My aim in doing this was to prove women were capable of conducting special forces roles, and indeed any combat related roles from which we were currently excluded. Having men and women trained the same improved military capability and capacity. It also would increase our effectiveness in engaging with civilian populations. I had proved my point. Or had I?

9 - NOT READY FOR CHANGE

My euphoria at having passed faded quickly when the Commander of Special Forces announced that no more women would be allowed to attempt the selection course! I could not believe my ears! Why would he want to stop a cadre of capable and competent women attempting the selection course when we had just proved we could do it? Why would you stop being able to access 50% of the talent of the Australian population? I never got answers to why the sudden change in policy. My theory is that we had created a serious problem by passing the course. The Commander wrongly assumed that all three women would fail. I expect his plan was to say, 'See? We tried. All the women failed, so now let's get back to how we used to do business.' It was at this point I believe the ADF missed an enormous opportunity to make these impactful policy changes - to be a world leader with women employed in all combat related roles.

Unfortunately, Australia had to wait until we had a female Prime Minister. Julia Gillard ensured the policy changed and opened up all combat roles to women. This was 15 years later, in 2014! What a waste of time, talent and capability!

Because I had passed the Commando Selection course my Commander could not stop me from progressing. Unfortunately, the other two women, who were Reservists, were not approved by their Commanders to conduct further courses, so their path to a Green Beret was stopped in its tracks! It was now critical that I qualify for the Green Beret. It was now totally up to me. I knew I would be under the closest scrutiny from both special forces and the wider military. There was no way I could afford to fail. I pinned my ears back and did course after course.

The first was the parachute course. Again, I was the only woman on the course. There were soldiers qualifying for a position as a paratrooper in the 3rd Parachute Battalion, special forces personnel, and navy clearance divers. I recall being in awe of one of the navy clearance divers. Extremely capable, he picked up the new parachute techniques we were being taught immediately. He could execute the perfect 'para roll' when we practised our parachute landing fall so we would not injure ourselves. We also practised how to manoeuvre in the sky and avoid running into each other's parachutes. This would not be good, our Instructor grimly told us. You would both go straight down very fast and we would need to clean up the mess. It would not be pretty!

We practised our drills in a suspended parachute harness. Four nylon risers or cords connected our harness to the parachute canopy. Our drills consisted of pulling our own body weight up the risers. We did these drills again and again, drill after drill, until we could do it in our sleep. Our hands were blistered from this relentless training. Men started dropping out as they injured themselves during these drills. It was another tough course where only the strong and determined survived.

We were so excited when the day finally arrived for us to do a real parachute jump. This was when I remembered I was scared of heights. Oh well, too bad. We boarded the C130 Hercules and sat on the floor of the aircraft, in line behind one another. We were 'clean skinned' - no equipment or weapons. When the countdown came, we stood up, and in an orderly fashion we exited the aircraft, one by one. I did not think of my fear of heights, just the drills we had learnt. A course mate of mine was not thinking about his drills. Suddenly he crashed through my risers and into my parachute. I immediately thought of what our Instructor had predicted if this very thing should happen. He should have spread his arms and legs, turned his head and bounced off my parachute, as per the drill. I quickly started to separate my risers so he could get out. We would hit the ground together very soon if I could not get rid of him. This would likely be fatal, or at least end my career through severe injury. 'Get out of my fuckin' parachute!' I yelled. Then suddenly he was gone and my parachute began to stabilise. The ground was rushing up, so now I had to remember my parachute landing fall. I had broken one bone and I never wanted to break another one.

I turned my parachute into the wind and landed on the ground so lightly that I was still standing up. Looking around I saw my course mates coming in quickly and doing their parachute rolls, some better than others. Expletives punctuated the air where there was a heavier fall. Well, I suppose I had better do one too. I slowly rolled forward and did a perfect dainty parachute roll and immediately started packing up my parachute as we were trained. Parachuting was just our method of entry; we then had to be prepared to conduct any number of tasks, all of which would probably involve a long hot walk. Suddenly an ambulance raced past me onto the drop zone. It turned out the clearance diver who I had so admired had 'speared in' and had a serious compound fracture to his leg. We never saw him again. However, it certainly focussed the rest of us on perfecting our landing techniques. Two other members who ended up in trees and injured themselves were also removed from the course.

By the end of the course we were sufficiently competent to do a parachute jump at night, with all our battle equipment and our weapon. As we neared the ground, we would lower our pack and weapon by a rope. Our equipment would hit the ground first and then we would land right near it and quickly grab our weapon so we were ready to fight whilst we packed up our parachute. More were injured, some by landing on their equipment, some forgetting to release their equipment and landing very heavily. A sprain here, a break there. Again, the course numbers were reduced.

I passed the parachute course and received my airborne wings. One by one I completed the courses required to become a commando. I was told that I passed them well, in the top 5%. I was chuffed to hear that, although I suspected the Commander of Special Operations was not so happy. Although the male dominated leadership was not ready for change, I found the men doing the courses were totally accepting of me. The fact that I was a woman was never an issue. We just all got on and did the training together as equals. I enjoyed training alongside these professional and capable men. I trust they recognised how seamlessly we worked together as we conducted these arduous and challenging courses.

I hoped that when they became senior leaders, decision makers, and maybe even the Commander Special Forces, they would make different decisions to that of the current Commander. They had been given the opportunity to see working with women as normal and a change for the better! They often joked that it was easy to spot two male special forces operatives in the field - two strong beefy blokes with big watches and black backpacks. A man and woman operative could easily pose as a touristy looking couple who would blend in. Our differences are our strength.

I felt immensely proud when I finally received the coveted Green Beret in 1999. I knew I had achieved a monumental milestone. The next morning I came to work wearing my Green Beret. The airborne wings on the sleeve of my uniform had been replaced with the green commando wings - commonly called the 'green moth.' I was one of a kind. I became used to seeing the surprised reactions of people. They would look twice to check if they had really seen a Green Beret and wings on a woman!

I was already at Headquarters Special Operations located on Garden Island, Sydney for a two year posting. I was determined to do a great job, to prove that women can operate in this environment just as well as the men. As the first woman to wear a Green Beret in the ADF, I was going to make sure that I would not be the last, despite the current ruling holding women back.

Receiving my Green Beret

10 – MISSED OPPORTUNITIES

In 1999, there was a lot of activity happening on Australia's doorstep in East Timor. It would prove a busy time for our group and the military in general. There was a large and rapid deployment of elements of the ADF, including special forces who deployed as part of International Force East Timor (INTERFET). INTERFET was a multinational peacemaking task force, organised and led by Australia to help stabilise East Timor after it gained independence from Indonesia in 1999. The East Timorese had suffered terribly under the Indonesian rule since 1975. The Task Force was commanded by Major General Peter Cosgrove, later to become the Chief of Army, then the Chief of Defence Force and ultimately Governor General of Australia.

The 4th Battalion Royal Australian Regiment (later retitled the 2nd Commando Regiment), was preparing to go to East Timor as part of INTERFET. Their Commanding Officer suggested that I talk to my Career Advisor and organise to become the next Officer Commanding of their supporting Signal Squadron, 126 Signal Squadron (Commando). He said, 'You have the experience and the knowledge of special operations and I would be very happy for you to command our communications squadron in East Timor.' I was elated that he had such confidence in my ability. I now held the rank of Major, and was of the seniority to command a squadron. Why not a Commando Signals Squadron? I could definitely do the job and do it well. I informed my Career Advisor, who was responsible for managing my career and postings, of the Commanding Officer's request. My Career Advisor gave it the thumbs down, with no explanation. To this day I don't know the reason. A male officer was posted into the role instead of me. I was devastated and very angry!

It was constantly blowing my mind that these decision makers could not see the opportunities passing them by. This was another 'sliding door' moment. It could have been the start of beret qualified women serving in mainstream special forces roles. It would have set the conditions for other women to follow. It wasn't just about me - I knew there were many women - far more capable, competent and talented than myself - who could fulfil these roles. Again, the opportunity for change was foiled by the short sightedness of decision makers.

Towards the end of my time at Headquarters Special Operations, I was invited to join an expedition to climb to the summit of Mount McClintock in Antarctica - the highest peak in Australian Territory - to celebrate the Centenary of Federation in early 2001. Mount McClintock is 3490 metres tall - half as high again as Mount Kosciuszko, the highest peak on the Australian mainland. We were going to be the first to climb Mount McClintock. Unfortunately, our expedition leader was warned by Dick Smith that the Americans would try and climb Mount McClintock first. Nevertheless, we commenced our preparation and started training.

As a Communications Officer, my job was to organise

the satellite communications for the expedition. We did our climbing training on the Three Sisters in the Blue Mountains. I had never done rock climbing before, due to my fear of heights. If I was honest, I did not really like being cold either. Being a member of this team meant I would need to overcome my fear of heights and get used to operating in a cold climate. The expedition leader took it upon himself to teach me how to rock climb. We finished one climb at night and in the middle of a storm so I had some cold weather experience too. I was as ready as I would ever be.

Then bad news struck! The Americans had reached the summit of Mount McClintock before we could get there. Some American geologists and their guides had **flown** high up onto Mount McClintock, via helicopter, from their nearby base camp and walked the final bit to the top. Not really a climb, but Australia's highest peak was no longer untouched. There was a rumour that the American expedition had cheekily left a bottle of champagne at the summit for us. Disappointed, our leader cancelled the expedition. Another missed opportunity!

I then learned I would assume command of another signals squadron at Victoria Barracks in Paddington, Sydney. As usual, I picked myself up, brushed myself off and did what I was told. This was a great location, surrounded by so much history. I was going make the most of this posting and ensure I enjoyed every minute of it. I relished the opportunity to run my own show and avoid the mistakes I had observed other commanders make. These experiences had taught me that 'a fish rots from its head'. My objective was to avoid this - to do the right thing by my subordinates as well as my superiors. People are our best assets and need to be valued and supported – which I did. An opportunity not missed!

The following year, in 2002, I was sent to East Timor as part of the UN Transitional Administration in East Timor (UNTAET). INTERFET had been successful and now the UN was running the mission to oversee the independence process for the East Timorese people. My new job was overseeing the Communications and Information Systems for the Australian contingent. For once, I was in the right place at the right time!

*East Timor - right place, right time.
About to board a huge UN helicopter.*

Not long into my tour in East Timor, Lieutenant General Peter Cosgrove the Chief of Army, was visiting the Australian contingent's base. I heard him telling his Regimental Sergeant Major to "Find that female Commando, I want to meet her". I walked over and said, 'Sir, I believe you are looking for me'. He congratulated me on achieving the Green Beret. I said, 'I hope I am not the last woman to wear a green beret.' There was a pause and he said, 'Aaahhh. Well, we will see'. I could tell by his tone that nothing would change. It was deeply disappointing to realise he was missing an opportunity. As the Chief of Army, he had the power to change the policy. The Commander Special Forces worked for him. One phone call would have done it!

Our senior leadership, most of whom had served in the Vietnam War, could not, or would not, see the potential of women serving in all combat related roles, including special forces. There appeared to be a generational, organisational and cultural block to change. There is always risk associated with any change, and it appeared the leadership did not want to accept this risk. I knew from experience that there was very little willingness to allow women to conduct the special forces selection course, even after three women had passed it! You either pass or you don't. There is no distinction between male and female. So where was the risk? Where was the visionary leadership? Why were the Generals so resistant to change? What were they afraid of? I believe they did not recognise, or did not care about, the opportunity Australia had here. We could have been world leaders in the employment of women in the military!

11 – AN OPPORTUNITY NOT MISSED

Since my experience in Bougainville, I had been aware that there were always vulnerable people after a conflict. These people always needed a helping hand. Whilst still in East Timor an opportunity came knocking that I would not miss.

My team and I were working hard to successfully deliver the communications support that was required of us, when I was approached by the Communications Officer from the UN Headquarters. He wanted me to help him with a UN task, setting up satellite dishes across the country, in the more remote and hard to access regions. The satellite dishes would allow these isolated villagers to watch the historic Independence Day Ceremony and elaborate celebrations in the capital, Dili. This would be an extraordinary event after years of conflict and hardship. I asked him why the UN Force Communications Unit was not able to do this job themselves, since it was their role. He just rolled his eyes, saying it needed to be done quickly - the big day was just around the corner.

I had quickly discovered how bad the roads were in East Timor and how difficult it was to move around. I knew from experience that the movement of vulnerable people in a country recovering from conflict can be difficult and dangerous. Armed militias of desperate young men roamed the countryside. I had already experienced an ambush by several young men armed with machetes. I was travelling through a remote region in a vehicle with a civilian Telstra technician to check a satellite dish. We were driving slowly on a muddy, treacherous road when a tree suddenly fell in front of our vehicle blocking the road. Armed men leapt out of hiding. One yanked open the driver's door, yelling for the technician to hand over his money or he would be killed. One of the men leaned aggressively into the vehicle and saw me in the passenger seat. I calmly reached across and pulled my shirt back to reveal the pistol on my hip. His eyes widened as he realised a pistol trumped a machete. He slammed the door and barked an order. The men quickly dragged the fallen tree off the road and let us pass. Experiences like this meant I would travel by helicopter when I could, but this was not an option for the villagers in these remote regions. Going to Dili was not possible for these people, so I knew if we did not help them get the satellite dishes they would miss out on seeing the celebrations that were so important for their new country.

Although it was not strictly our mission, it would be an important 'hearts and minds' contribution to our stabilisation operation. Now all I had to do was convince my Commander that we needed to do this, and do it quickly. The clock was ticking.

As expected, the Commander was not happy. However, he begrudgingly gave his approval on the one understanding that if anything went wrong with our own communications in the meantime, I would be 'fired' and on the first plane back to Australia. It was worth the risk. I briefed my team that the Commander had approved the task, omitting the piece that if we were not successful in balancing this new project with our other day-to-day tasks, my head would be on the chopping block. My team members were ecstatic to get out of Dili and achieve a task that they could see brought both short term and long-term communications access to these remote villages. The UN had agreed to my condition that the satellite dishes would stay in place to provide the villagers with ongoing communications and reduce their sense of isolation. It was a win-win situation.

On the helicopter before heading out on the task

Fortunately for me, it all went to plan and I wasn't sent home. My team successfully installed the satellite dishes, so those isolated communities, men, women and children, enjoyed watching the fantastic Independence Day celebrations broadcast from Dili. We had the resources, we had the will and we grasped the opportunity with both hands to help those who could not help themselves. The remoteness and the poor infrastructure from 24 years of Indonesian rule had been circumstances well beyond their control or capacity. It was an opportunity seized.

12 – WHY TRAIN WOMEN?

Simultaneously, in other war-torn parts of the world, we were learning the importance of training women as part of security forces. In those affected Islamic countries, enemy soldiers were dressing up as pregnant women. Wrapped in explosives, strolling unsearched through check points, these suicide bombers were causing horrific carnage, simply because of the cultural imperative that only women can search women!

Cleaning my weapon in Iraq while my team check communications equipment

Following Australia's involvement in East Timor and the invasion of Iraq in 2003, Australian combat troops were sent back to Iraq on Operation Catalyst and took responsibility for supporting Iraqi security forces in one of the southern provinces. In August 2006 I welcomed my deployment to Iraq for seven months. The Australian Headquarters was based at Camp Victory, an American base in the capital, Baghdad. Our Headquarters was located in one of Saddam Hussein's hunting lodges - a surreal experience in itself. My role was the senior communications officer for the Australian contingent, with technical control over 120 communicators across five countries. Having now been promoted to Lieutenant Colonel, I was well prepared for and revelled in this demanding role.

On a planning task in Afghanistan

Moving critical communications equipment in Afghanistan

The security situation was very tense. We received frequent attacks, with rockets being fired indiscriminately into Camp Victory - killing people who were unfortunately in the wrong place at the wrong time.

My job meant that I often travelled throughout our huge Area of Operations. For example, I travelled to Afghanistan for three weeks to conduct communications planning to prepare for an influx of Australian troops in the future. On another occasion, I took a two person briefing team, on behalf of my Commander, to welcome the new ship HMAS TOOWOOMBA to the Persian Gulf. Her role was to replace HMAS WARRAMUNGA and continue conducting maritime security operations. The briefing team and I were responsible for ensuring the ship's new Commander and staff were well prepared for their tour of duty. I volunteered for the job as

I had not been on many ships since I sailed to Bougainville many years before. I also wanted to see the ship that was named after the city where I was born.

In early November 2006 Saddam Hussein was sentenced to death for crimes against humanity by an Iraqi Tribunal. There was a lot of shooting in the air by those Iraqis who were happy with the verdict. Unfortunately, what goes up must come down. Several civilians and American soldiers had been killed by returning bullets from the sky which struck them in the head - from both inside and outside of buildings. Our Commander immediately announced an upgrade of our personal protection. We were to wear helmet and body armour indoors and out during these celebrations.

I rang a friend in Australia from the cramped phone booth inside the headquarters. It was not designed to accommodate me in all my body armour. She immediately wanted to talk about what she was seeing on the TV news about events in Baghdad. I said, 'Yes, most Iraqis seem happy with the verdict, but that's not why I am ringing you. Can you please put a box trifecta on these three horses in the Melbourne Cup?' The silence on the other end of the phone was deafening!

Aside from my successful flutter on the Melbourne Cup, my job continued to keep me busy. The daily briefings were peppered with horrifying reports of male enemy suicide bombers dressing up as women, with explosives strapped to their stomachs. These 'women' were then able to get through the military checkpoints manned by Iraqi security forces. Once past the checkpoint, they would blow themselves up along with their military and civilian targets. This was possible because there were no women trained in the Iraqi security forces to conduct searches of these 'women', a critical gap in their capability as culturally only women could search women. The enemy was using this to their advantage.

The Taliban were also using this effective tactic in Afghanistan. Australia troops had been in Afghanistan on Operation Slipper since 2001 as part of a Coalition force. The Taliban were also hiding explosives under burqas, and getting through checkpoints. Again the cultural imperatives preventing men from searching women, appeared to be the primary impediment in both operational areas.

As part of my role in Iraq, I oversaw the fitting out of our vehicles with Counter Improvised Explosive Device equipment to protect our forces. I had seen plenty of vehicles hit by Improvised Explosive Devices and seen the effect of such explosions on vehicles and human bodies. I received a video of CCTV footage taken in Afghanistan, sent to me as part of the daily briefings. It featured an Afghan man walking towards the camera followed by a woman, smaller and submissively bowed over. The man looked directly into the camera then turned around and shot the woman, probably either his wife, sister or daughter, in the head. He then laughed at the camera and walked off. It was wantonly done to make a perverse point! It was about control, about power and dominance.

That particular vision stayed with me for a long time. That simple act of the Afghan man killing a woman and laughing made me profoundly angry. She was vulnerable and totally unprotected. That man was supposed to be her protector, and he shot her. There was **no** safety net for her, **no** protection, and **no** justice. I felt strongly that we should support both these countries, Iraq and Afghanistan, to help them to build their own effective security forces. This would in turn provide a safe and secure environment for the civilian population, in particular the women and girls. To achieve this, they would need women as an integral part of their security forces.

I left Iraq satisfied I had conducted my communications role well and set the conditions for my successor to continue the important work we were doing. I had also passed an important milestone of 20 years in service and I knew I was at a crossroads in my career. I had an important decision to make.

13 – TOO MUCH CHANGE

Whilst in Iraq, I began to consider whether it was time to leave the full time Army. Ironically, I started thinking about this on Armistice Day 2006, my 20th anniversary of joining up. After all this time I felt that I was on top of my game. I had served to the best of my ability. I had broken the rules and long held beliefs for so long. I had made change where I could. Now it was somebody else's turn.

I had reached my ceiling rank. I had not been selected to become a Commanding Officer of a Regiment, and therefore was not eligible for the rank of full Colonel. My current rank of Lieutenant Colonel was as high as I could go. I had always maintained that I would retire whilst I was enjoying myself. I would step aside and let the younger officers come through. It was certainly not a sad realisation as I had thoroughly enjoyed my service. I had seen far too many people leave the

Serving in Iraq - starting to think if it was time to leave the Army

Army 'bitter and twisted' against the Army's leadership and management, and I did not want that to happen to me.

When I arrived home from Iraq, Mum hosted a celebration for my return, as she always did. I recall sitting there watching Dad throughout the evening, and realised that I was no longer watching him with fear or trepidation. At the end of the evening, after Mum had gone to bed, I did something I had wanted to do since I was a child. I walked up to my father and stood upright, tall and unafraid, in front of him. I asked him why he had bashed Mum for all those years. For the first time he looked back at me without his usual confidence. He said, 'I was trying to protect you girls from her.' I could not believe my ears! For all those years he had created an environment constantly punctuated by fear and violence. We had never known if an angry Dad would walk in the door, forcing us girls to escape out the windows while, invariably, he would take out his anger on Mum. She never ran away, but I'll bet she wanted to. She stayed trying to protect us from him! I said, 'Are you really serious, Dad? Mum never wanted to hurt us. **You** hurt Mum and **you** hurt us.' He stared back. Silent. No response. No remorse. No regret. No apology. And that was the end of my relationship with my father. I walked away. I walked out of his life.

The next day I told Mum what had happened. Forewarned is forearmed, I always say. I told her she could come and live with me, but she said her place was with Dad. I told her I was only a phone call away. I came to visit Mum frequently, to check on her. If Dad was there, I would say a polite 'Hello' and that was it. Almost immediately Dad would start attacking Mum verbally. I would put down my cup of coffee, say goodbye to Mum and leave, as hard as that was to do.

Dad told Mum that Iraq changed me. He was right. It had given me the courage to stand up to this violent man. I had to become a war veteran before I had the strength to stand up to him. It was sad it had taken that long. I remained estranged from him until his death.

I launched into upskilling myself for my next career. I completed a personal training course and a remedial massage course. In 2009 I started a Health and Fitness business from home in Ravensbourne, north of Toowoomba. Having been born in Toowoomba, I always felt an immense relief whenever I drove up the Range. My shoulders, which would be tucked up around my ears with stress, would relax and my mind would be at peace. I knew I was home.

The new business owner of Maximize Health

After I had left home and joined the Army, my parents had sold their farm in Highfields, and moved to another beautiful farm in Ravensbourne, growing avocados and raising beef cattle. For the first time in a long while I would be close enough to give Mum some of the support she so richly deserved.

While I was in the Army, I had tried to instigate change in the organisation with limited success. It was time for me to take control of my own life now. I wanted to be my own boss. Although I felt I had made the right decision to leave the full time Army, I continued to serve in the Army Reserve. I was not ready to cut the umbilical cord yet!

I had been in uniform for 22 years, serving since I was seventeen years old - the only work I had known as an adult. Now I was working seven days a week, putting in long, long days to establish my new business. It was successful. However, it was bloody hard work - starting boot camp at 0500 hours, seeing clients for personal training and swimming sessions and giving massages late into the evening. I was missing the camaraderie and mateship of the Army - being part of the 'green machine'. My body continued to hurt every day too. I had developed chronic pain from my military service - headaches, a sore neck, back, knees and of course my ankle!

This is what brought me to the stage where I had the 'Death Tree' experience described earlier. I had never thought, for one moment, that I was a person who would ever contemplate committing suicide. I was a person who had navigated a sea of change and always been positive. I was mentally and physically tough. I had been trained to 'suck it up', 'grit my teeth' and soldier on no matter how much it hurt. Now I was no longer in the full time Army there was a feeling of disconnectedness - of mental isolation. Leaving the Army had more of an impact on me than actually being in the Army!

At work in my gym

Reflecting back on my tours of duty, I recalled many occasions when I believed I would lose my life. I once thought I would be raped and killed by young men disenfranchised by a conflict. I had experienced missiles and rockets constantly crashing into my location, sometimes sleeping in my helmet and body armour because they were landing so close. A missile had locked onto the plane I was in, forcing it to disperse chaff (tiny decoy flares) to confuse the missile. Simultaneously the pilot veered the plane sharply out of harm's way. On all these occasions I thought my time was up. I was not scared of dying. I knew when my time was up, it was up. My faith had taught me how to live life and how to die, both with calmness and confidence. Narrowly escaping death, and having time to contemplate it, gives you a different perspective - a positive perspective. Life is short. Don't waste time!

I realised that killing myself that night would not have been a solution to my problems. Mum would have been dreadfully upset and she also would have been angry at my decision. As Christians, Mum and I had similar beliefs. We believed the Lord decides on the time, manner and place of our death and therefore this was not my decision to make. I was reminded that life was precious, not to be squandered away on a selfish whim. We were put on this earth for a reason. That faith - that belief in something higher than me - saved me from myself.

Soon after my interlude with the 'Death Tree' - my wakeup call for the need to change - a friend told me about a therapy that helps with chronic pain caused by musculoskeletal misalignment. That sounded exactly like what I needed. Ever since I had broken my ankle at officer training, 20 years earlier, I suffered chronic pain from head to toe. I drove two hours to Redcliffe to see Kym Finch, the founder of Finch

Therapy. Forty-five minutes later, I walked out from my first appointment, pain free! I could not believe I could be pain free after all those years! I was able to sleep without putting a pillow under my knees. Miraculously, the chronic body pain and headaches had vanished.

When I went back a week later to see Kym for my follow-up appointment, I asked her if she would train me. This she did over the next 12 months and, thanks to Kym, I was then able to remodel my business. I became a Finch Therapist and focused on alleviating chronic pain through musculoskeletal alignment. My patients were so happy with the relief they experienced that soon their friends were coming from all over Queensland to see me. Finch Therapy worked for me and it worked for my patients. Most of them were women who were suffering chronic pain after childbirth or injury. I loved helping my patients experience that same freedom from chronic pain I had felt. A world without chronic pain is like being given a new lease on life. My world was good!

However, another big change was about to descend on the family. Late in 2014, Dad was diagnosed with a metastatic melanoma, a severe form of skin cancer which rapidly spread to his brain and lungs. Ironically, Mum had constantly reminded Dad about sun protection. She would follow him out the door holding up the sunscreen and a long-sleeved shirt asking, 'Mike, please put some sunscreen on.' But Dad always knew best.

When he became ill, Mum, with the help of family, cared for him at home until he died. Her niece, Ute, flew out from

Germany to help. It was two months and two days from diagnosis to death. Mum was able to take control soon after he was diagnosed. She sat her four girls down and told us exactly what she wanted to happen, and we got on with it. My job was to help prepare and sell their hundred head of cattle to help pay down Dad's debts. Mum had sensibly allocated me an outside job not involved in the nursing of Dad.

I know Mum missed him, but I was thankful he had died before Mum. She had two years of peace without him.

14 - INITIATING CHANGE – WOMEN, PEACE AND SECURITY

After Dad died I recommenced my business at home and continued to serve as an Army reservist. I had a constant feeling that there was more work to be done in Afghanistan. I started to hope I would be asked to go back there in the future. I had never forgotten the CCTV footage of the Afghan man shooting that defenceless woman! It was etched in my mind. I wanted to go to Afghanistan and help where I could.

I had now been running my business for seven years. Anticipating change, I spoke to Anna, my business manager, who I had introduced after my Death Tree incident. I was now sharing the workload of running the business instead of trying to do it all myself. It was working. I could focus on my Finch patients. In preparation, Anna and I workshopped a scenario should I ever happen to get the call to deploy again. As a reservist I was still able to serve if required. We determined I would be able to close my business and restart it on my return. I did not realise how timely our planning was!

One week later, just before Christmas, I received a phone call offering me a position in Afghanistan for nine months. I was over the moon! This was exactly what I wanted. I was mentally ready to go back to a war zone. They wanted me to be in Afghanistan in three weeks' time! I had to move fast. Due to previous planning, I was able to quickly advise my patients and recommend who they should see in my absence.

In January 2015, I landed in the smog filled capital, Kabul. Our base was surrounded by tall blast walls and protective concrete walls, with heavy security, steel barricades, tyre spikes and checkpoints. Because Kabul is located 1800 metres above sea level, the air is thin and the city is covered in a layer of thick smog. Kabul is one of the most polluted cities in the world and rates up there with cities like New Delhi or Beijing. Afghans burn anything to stay warm in winter including tyres and even faeces, so you are literally breathing in shit! That was the smell that entered my nostrils when I landed - burning rubber and rubbish!

The first thing I noticed was the fatigue of the United States (US) military - they were exhausted from having been the heavy lifters of the campaign against terrorism in Afghanistan for the last 15 years. As an example, my boss was on his eighth tour of duty in Afghanistan, and it had cost him his family life. His staff were so worried that they were trying to get his pistol confiscated from him for fear he would turn it on them. They were unsuccessful. I spent a lot of time talking with him, and gained the impression that he was understandably burnt out and just needed to go home.

My job was the Senior Lessons Learnt Staff Officer in the Resolute Support Mission, now a North Atlantic Treaty Organisation (NATO) mission. The mission had started because of 9/11, when coalition forces had gone after Osama Bin Laden, and the operation appeared to be still run by the United States.

The Taliban rule had been removed by the coalition forces

and conditions had improved for women and girls with the dumping of the Taliban's hard-line interpretation of Islam. The women's freedom of movement and the ability to access their humanitarian rights had improved. The changes had been embraced by the women - the people affected the most. I recall an Australian Commander recently describing these years in Afghanistan as, 'Although it was not the land of milk and honey it was a vast improvement to what their life was like under Taliban rule'. We did not know then that, sadly, it was not to be a lasting change.

Running a Lessons Learnt meeting in Kabul

I was working in the Mission Headquarters in the Afghanistan Assessment Group in the Planning Branch. It was an insightful job. In the business I had just left, I used to assess human beings for chronic pain. Now I was assessing what we had learnt in this violent drawn-out conflict. I received a report from a US special forces unit as they were leaving Afghanistan after their 12-month tour. The report concluded that the biggest impediment to the successful conduct of their operations had been that they did not understand the Afghan people. I was gobsmacked! After nearly 15 years of conflict and working with the Afghan people, this was still the case? It puzzled me immensely. Clearly the coalition forces needed to engage more proactively, in order to improve their understanding of the Afghan people and their culture.

I was approached by an Australian Colonel, Amanda Fielding, who was the mission's Senior Gender Advisor. The mission had Gender Advisers! Wow! This was the first time I was formally introduced to the term 'Women, Peace and Security' (WPS). The US Security Council Resolution 1325 had been signed off in 2000. Military Gender Advisors were now being employed to ensure Resolution 1325 was being integrated as part of the mission. This ensured women were trained effectively as part of the security forces - the army and the police. Based on what I had learnt on my previous tours of duty overseas, this made perfect sense to me.

Colonel Fielding was a professional and exceptionally competent officer, effectively advising the Afghan Ministry of Defence and Ministry of Interior to safely integrate women within their forces, including into their training institutions. Colonel Fielding asked if I could assist her with conducting workshops with women from the Afghan National Army.

These workshops were designed to assist the Afghan National Army develop strategies for the recruiting and retention of women, whilst always maintaining the security of these women. I could see first-hand the operational necessity of this. In an Islamic Afghan society, it was a cultural imperative. With no hesitation I accepted Colonel Fielding's challenge.

Along with her Gender Advisor Cell, I worked with the Afghan National Army women - amazing and strong women focused on helping their country achieve peace and security. They said they wanted to stand shoulder to shoulder – 'shona ba shona' - with the men to defend their country against the Taliban. The women initially were focused on recruiting. However, I suggested that if they focused on their retention strategies, their recruiting issues would start to resolve themselves. Look after the people you already have.

One of the reasons they lost a lot of women was the lack of facilities that would allow for women's safety in their work place. Separate toilets, change facilities and accommodation were essential. It seemed that 'segregation enables integration' in Afghanistan. Half way through her deployment Colonel Fielding had visited an Afghan National Army Corps in the north of Afghanistan. Her role included ensuring international funds were being spent properly. In this case she needed to ensure both men and women were provided with appropriate separate living and working accommodation in accordance with cultural requirements. What she discovered was the men were living in the brand-new accommodation and the 20 women were living next to the dog kennels in one shipping container with one blocked up Porta-loo between them! Nobody thought this was wrong as the women were at least safely away from the men. Colonel Fielding soon fixed that!

Working with Colonel Fielding. What a team!

Colonel Fielding and her team engaging with Afghanistan National Army women at the Officer Academy. They have been blurred out for security reasons.

I left the Headquarters in Kabul in early October 2015, flying in a British military helicopter to Hamid Karzai International Airport to head home after a long nine months. I was feeling so emotional. Waves of sadness engulfed me. I felt tears welling up in my eyes. Although I felt I had achieved a lot, there was still so much work to be done for the Afghan women and girls. I felt like I was deserting them, when they still needed a helping hand. An Australian soldier I knew was sitting opposite me. He must have noticed the pain on my face as I stared silently down at the city rushing by. He said jovially, 'Hey Ma'am, I hope we don't get another missile lock like last week. How scary was that!' I looked up at him, happy for the distraction. I said to the soldier, 'Yes, I am glad this is my last chopper ride for a while.' He laughed and agreed, both of us relieved to be heading home.

The previous week we had both been in a British Puma helicopter that had survived a missile lock from a Taliban Surface to Air weapon. This was a dangerous new tactic being employed by the Taliban. Helicopters are notorious for flying 'low and slow', hence were vulnerable to being shot down by a missile. The helicopter pilots had immediately gone straight up, gaining altitude very rapidly to evade the missile. The soldier and I had been sitting together, both watching with concern as the Loadmaster dashed from one side of the helicopter to other, peering down and around us. I gathered he was looking for a missile on our tail. The soldier and I turned and looked silently at each, both calm, but with very wide eyes and raised eyebrows. We both started to become breathless as the air became thin because we had gone so high. Fortunately, the Loadmaster seemed happy the missile threat was gone at that point and we started to descend.

Several days later, when I was safely back in Australia, a British Puma helicopter clipped a communications-balloon tethering cable with its rotor blade as it came to pick up passengers at our Kabul base. It lost control and crashed into the small landing zone. There were five people killed and five people injured in the crash. Unfortunately, one of those killed was the female US Gender Advisor from Southern Command - a key member of the Gender Advisor team. Another sad day and huge loss to the mission.

Having safely completed my tour of duty in Afghanistan, I returned to Australia and reopened my clinic the next day. My patients had obviously put my return date in their diaries and the phone started ringing. Whilst I was enjoying helping my patients again, I knew there was more work I could do to help women and girls around the world. Several months later, the phone rang. It was Colonel Fielding! She asked if I wanted to come to Canberra to help her integrate the Women, Peace and Security Resolution into the ADF's planning for operations and exercises. Her mission was to ensure the ADF deliberately considered a gender perspective into all its operational planning processes. A no-brainer for me! As much as I loved my business, I knew I could contribute to her mission. I thought it was important meaningful, so I happily said 'Yes!' to her again.

I packed up my business more permanently this time. Even though Colonel Fielding could only promise me a 12-month contract, I took the risk and this time did not give my patients a return date. I felt as though a chapter was closing and another one was opening. It was a great feeling, even though I had no idea what to expect. I packed up and headed back to Canberra, ready to roll up my sleeves and get busy. And boy it was busy! I thought running my own business was hectic - but our feet barely hit the ground for the next 18 months.

We were fortunate that our Commander, Vice Admiral David Johnston (currently Deputy to the Chief of Defence Forces), recognised the work we were doing was adding value to his mission and he supported our endeavours. This was a game changer for us. Support from 'the top' made it much easier to achieve our goals

Three weeks after I arrived in frosty Canberra, Colonel Fielding sent me to warm Fiji to complete a Women, Peace and Security activity to find out how effectively the ADF had responded to Tropical Cyclone (TC) Winston and how we could do better next time. TC Winston was the most intense tropical cyclone in the Southern Hemisphere to date, having killed 44 people, and inflicted extensive damage across Fiji. Operation Fiji Assist was the first time the ADF had specifically employed Gender Advisers as part of the Government's response. The Gender Advisors acquitted themselves well and added value to the mission.

As I had first experienced in Bougainville, and as the

Working in Fiji on a planning exercise, complete with commando wings

Gender Advisors demonstrated, when women talked to the affected women, they were more likely to find out exactly what the women, children and vulnerable people in the community needed for their recovery. You would not always get that information by talking only to the men.

I learnt later that there were other, longer lasting, effects from our operation in Fiji. In 2019, I was talking to a Fijian Captain in Brisbane. He told me he had been on Korro Island, Fiji, when the ADF arrived to support the Fijian Military and the affected communities clean up and rebuild after TC Winston. His observation was that when Australian military women arrived, flying helicopters, driving boats, as engineers with chainsaws and axes - this was life changing for many girls on Korro Island. Those girls were now staying at school so they could become a pilot or an engineer like the Australian military women they saw. These girls now had role models – they could be what they could see.

Only a few short years later Fiji was able to reciprocate the assistance we had provided them after TC Winston. Australia was brought to its knees, during the 2019-2020 catastrophic bushfire season known as Black Summer - a megafire which killed 33 people. The fire affected countless lives and properties, burning 24 million hectares. The Fijian military, Bula Force, came and supported our response. They helped our communities as we had helped theirs. Vinaka, Bula Force - thank you!

Several months later Colonel Fielding sent me to Sweden, to the Nordic Centre for Gender in Military Operations to do the two-week Gender Advisor course. This was a wonderful experience for me as this is the centre of excellence for gender training and at the time was the only place in the world that trained Gender Advisors. Colonel Fielding had asked me to see what we could learn about how their Gender Advisor course was conducted. We had realised that in order to grow our capability we had to train our own Gender Advisors. It was cost prohibitive to send all our people to Sweden, especially given the number we had to prepare for our many operations and exercises. We needed our own course. The Swedish course was full on, but I managed to squeeze in a trip to see the ABBA Museum, a personal highlight.

With the support of the Nordic Centre, I came back from Sweden with a USB stick containing their course. It was a good course, but we needed to create an Australian version, focused on our region and our processes. Colonel Fielding conceptualised and led the development of the first Operational Gender Advisor course in the Southern Hemisphere. We were fortunate that Group Captain Dee Gibbon (who had replaced Colonel Fielding in Afghanistan and had a PHD in Gender in Defence), made herself available as an educator to write the course. We were also lucky to persuade the military Gender Advisor from the UN New York Headquarters, Lieutenant Colonel Rachel Grimes, a United Kingdom Army officer, to assist us with the course. Rachel was one of the first Military Gender Advisors to be posted to a UN Mission in Africa and had a wealth of knowledge. She was a real asset to us. We engaged widely with non-government organisations and civil society. It was not perfect, but it was an excellent start.

Interestingly, we had more men than women on that first course, as we targeted operational planners and intelligence staff from key Headquarters. That was the start. Colonel Fielding oversaw, with my eager assistance and input, the building of a strong network of operationally focused Gender Advisors both regionally and globally. This network could institute real change!

In July 2016, we heard a concerning report from the UN Mission in South Sudan. Troops from the Sudanese Peace Liberation Army, fresh from winning a battle with opposition troops, went on a wild rampage in the capital, Juba. One attack occurred just down the road from UN House, a large base where the Headquarters of the UN mission was located. Thousands of UN peacekeepers were located there. At least 15 Sudanese Peace Liberation Army soldiers' gang-raped three western women working for UN aid agencies in a compound only one kilometre up the road from the UN Headquarters. The peacekeepers and the US Embassy staff were criticised for not answering the repeated phone calls for help from the women, especially as they were so close. I was appalled! In what mission would a UN peacekeeper sit in a relatively safe compound and do nothing to assist women being gang-raped just up the road? Surely that was why they were there - to protect vulnerable people! I wanted to go to South Sudan right now! Clearly, change was much needed.

Earlier that year, the ADF had established a new Gender Advisor position in South Sudan as part of the small Australian military contingent in the UN mission. The current Gender Advisor there was due to be replaced soon, so I asked Colonel Fielding if she would make arrangements to send me to South Sudan as that replacement. Colonel Fielding promised she would pursue this, and we got back to work. I had sown the seed. I hoped it would grow.

15 - CHANGE FOR THE FAMILY

I relished watching Mum live her life free of the shackles of domestic violence - free from a life of constantly walking on eggshells. But we did not know that was to change far too soon.

In January 2017 Colonel Fielding sent me to the US to participate in Women, Peace and Security planning in Seattle. I had just finished giving a presentation on the planning considerations for a US and Australia Biennial Training Exercise. My audience was about 250 planning staff for this exercise. I was the last presentation for the day and received many interesting and challenging questions. As soon as I returned to my room on the Military Base where we were staying, I sat down and started making notes. I turned on my work phone and my personal phone, and continued writing responses to the questions I had received.

Suddenly both phones started vibrating and beeping, leaving message after message after message. I immediately knew something very bad must have happened. My heart started beating rapidly, my hands went clammy and I had a vision that my sister Tracy had been killed in a car crash! I grimly stared at the two noisy phones, too scared to pick them up. Which one should I answer first? I went for the work phone. It was a voice message from Colonel Fielding in Canberra. She sounded very upset. When I returned her call she told me my Mum had died in her sleep. She ordered me to fly home immediately and go on compassionate leave.

I felt as though I had been punched in the stomach. But I also felt relief that Mum had not suffered - dying in her sleep. She had received the dying grace she had earned as a mature spiritual believer. She had died just over two years after Dad - having had two years of peace. I wished it had been more! Mum died on Australia Day. She had always flown an Australian flag in her front yard, since the day she had become an Australian citizen. She was one of the most patriotic Australians I have ever known. That day my sister lowered her flag to half-mast.

Mum had blossomed in those two years. She had taken cattle in on agistment on her property so she could still enjoy watching cattle munching on the grass, but without the hassle of looking after them. Mum had also given up driving. This was not a bad thing as she had always been a notoriously slow driver. If I had ever come across a line of cars travelling slowly on the road to Toowoomba, I had a fair idea Mum would be right at the front! After she stopped driving she had employed a young local ex-special forces guy called Toby to be her chauffeur. Toby would fold himself into Mum's little Hyundai Getz, which we called Gerty, and drive her to Crows Nest so she could do shopping and attend appointments. Mum would cheekily say about her best friend, 'Margrit has a gardener but I have a chauffeur.'

Mum had told us she wanted to stay on the farm and said that if she got dementia (which she never did), just to build a tall fence so she could still go to the garden, but not wander off. When visitors came, which they frequently did, we were to make sure she looked presentable and pop some 'lippy' on her. Even today people talk about how much they enjoyed spending time with Mum, being spoilt with coffee and cake and chatting with an amazing woman.

Margrit had continued to take Mum to the Empire Theatre to watch the Camerata – Queensland's Chamber Orchestra, who were Mum's favourite musicians. They loved her too. At her funeral Brendan Joyce, Artistic Director and the violinist, played the 'Thais Meditation'. We kept this a secret in the lead up to the funeral. Margrit sobbed loudly when Brendon suddenly got up and played. Brendon later told us that he and his colleague talked about Mum all the way back to Brisbane after her funeral. She touched everyone who had the pleasure to meet her.

The chapel was packed with people inside and out. Mum had secretly paid for her and Dad's funerals at Burstow's Funeral Home - a few dollars a week for years - whenever she could surreptitiously

A photo of Mum that I carry with me.

put money aside. What a thoughtful and practical person she was! I was given the job of presenting the eulogy, which I compiled after much discussion and reflection. I was proud to be able to present this final tribute to my mother's amazing life.

I miss Mum dreadfully. She had always ensured that my sisters and I knew what was happening in the family. Mum was our family communications officer, our source of truth and information. She would individually ring us and tell us the news, remind us about birthdays – we were all kept in the loop. If we missed the call, she would leave a long, detailed message so we missed nothing. The only memento I asked for when Mum died was her Bible, because it had notes throughout in her lovely cursive hand writing.

A lot changed when Mum died. The all-informed family network Mum created disappeared but I was glad that she had finally been able to live the calm, peaceful life she deserved.

16 - A COUNTRY IN NEED OF CHANGE

I had learnt so much about Women, Peace and Security under the tutelage of Colonel Fielding. I was now a trained Military Gender Advisor and I was ready to go and apply this knowledge. I knew which country needed help - South Sudan.

In the middle of 2017, Colonel Fielding surprised me one day by saying, 'Start preparing. You are going to South Sudan in November.' Yessss! My wish had come true. I was ecstatic. Colonel Fielding and I handed over our current work load, our baby, to the new team and we took up new postings. Colonel Fielding stayed in Canberra and I went to Africa. We had started the large task of growing the ADF Gender Advisor capability - it was crawling and would need much more dedicated attention before it would be up and running or even walking. However, that was now somebody else's responsibility.

The plane landed in Entebbe, Uganda, 18 November 2017. After a few days of preparatory training, we flew into Juba, the capital of South Sudan. I was now a peacekeeper in the UN Mission in South Sudan (UNMISS). The mission consisted of peacekeepers from 47 countries and was the biggest UN mission in the world. The mission was established to support the new Republic of South Sudan as it recovered from 20 years of civil war between the Central Sudanese government and the Sudanese Peace Liberation Army (SPLA). In 2011 the Republic of South Sudan had become independent - the newest nation in the world. It should have been thriving, but wasn't. It was suffering from an internal civil war. As I stood under the trees and listened to the birds on my first day in Juba, I thought, 'Gee, even the birds sound sad!'

The situation was dire, especially for women and children, with rape and other forms of sexual violence being used as a tactic of war by both sides of the civil war. The 2017 statistics indicated that 60 percent of the sexual violence was committed by South Sudanese National security forces, with 97 percent of those violations committed against women and girls. My first task was to conduct a gender analysis to see where I could contribute to the mission's priorities - protection of civilians and enduring peace.

Initially I could not understand why the UN peacekeepers were not doing more to protect the population against this sexual violence. However, during my analysis I came to understand there was a complex political situation between the South Sudanese Government and the UN mission. This situation severely limited the ability of the peacekeepers to freely move about to conduct their engagement activities with the local population. These restrictions mostly confine peacekeeping patrols to the main supply routes and away from the civilian population where they were most needed – where the people were suffering sexual violence. That civilian protection task was the responsibility of the SPLA. Unfortunately, they were the perpetrators of the sexual violence, not the protectors!

This problem was further exacerbated by the fact that only 3.7 percent of the mission's peacekeepers were women. Few of those women were trained and therefore were not included in the protection patrols. For example, the Indian Battalion had no women, while the Nepalese Battalion had less than a dozen women trained for engagement tasks. These tasks could include sending an armed patrol to protect civilian women and girls while they collected firewood for cooking. If the women and girls were not protected, they were vulnerable to rape and being injured or killed. This was the high cost of being a woman in South Sudan!

The contents of my bedside safe in South Sudan - pistol, ammunition, US$1000 and lots of South Sudanese pounds. I felt like Pablo Escobar!

To make this terrible situation even worse, I discovered I was the only gender-trained and tasked staff officer in the military Headquarters of almost 14,000 military peacekeepers. Implementing gender considerations into the Mission's military planning and decision-making processes was going to be a huge job. It would be like eating an elephant, 'Take one bite at a time, and chew like crazy!' But I was the right person for the job, and I would need every bit of the military experience I had gained over the last thirty-three years. I took a deep breath, rolled up my sleeves and got to work.

I saw my first task in South Sudan as engaging with the women members of the SPLA. I met with Colonel Bol, an impressive woman and a very professional officer. Colonel Bol was from Dinka heritage and as such she towered over me at our first meeting, a situation that did not happen often. Colonel Bol was focused on helping her country get back on its feet, but she needed my assistance. She needed help to train the women currently in the military, so that they would be given more meaningful roles in the security of their country. The women needed to be educated on their constitutional rights and helped to gain skills that focused on empowering them. Colonel Bol spoke fluent Arabic and English and from our first meeting we developed a friendship based on our shared goals and shared sense of humour.

This empowerment was also a personal issue for Colonel Bol. Her good friend and fellow female officer had killed herself a few months earlier. Her friend expected that she would be kicked out of the military and would have no income to support her children. She and Colonel Bol had both lost their husbands in the conflict and now they faced another fight. There was no pension, no financial safety net for any of the women in the same dreadful situation. We now had a common goal - a mission to train and empower these women to ensure they could retain their meaningful employment. This change would need to come from within their ranks. Enough women had already died.

Flight Leiutenant Cook and me with Colonel Bol and her staff

Working with Colonel Bol

Colonel Bol wanted me to address the issues of human rights, South Sudanese law, international humanitarian laws, sexual and gender-based violence and sexual harassment in the work place. After listening intently to what Colonel Bol wanted, I designed and coordinated a three-day course using the expertise of people in the UN mission - the Rule of Law section, the Gender Affairs unit and the Senior Women's Protection Advisor. I also garnered external support from the South Sudanese Women's Lawyers Association and the South Sudan Women's Block - both valuable support groups. I gave the draft course syllabus to Colonel Bol for her consideration and approval. She was very impressed.

We now had to get approval from her leaders to conduct the course. The approving authority was a Major General whom she knew. Colonel Bol was well connected and we needed every connection to get this training off the ground. I told her that I would find a Major General to match her Major General. She laughed. However, we only had one Major General, the Deputy Commander of our military force. He was from Mongolia. I had to convince him this was a task worth starting - a task that had never been done before. I had done this before, trying to convince the leadership that change was necessary. This time it was serious. People's security and safety were on the line.

I briefed my Deputy Commander on the importance of training the SPLA women. I asked if he would come with me to meet the South Sudanese Major General to seek permission to conduct the course. Thankfully I was able to convince him, to the point where he was in enthusiastic agreement. It turned out that he had never been to the SPLA Headquarters and was keen to go. I could not believe that he had been in South Sudan for over a year without going there, whereas I had only been in the country for a month or two. The meeting went well and there was approval all round. Colonel Bol and I had permission to proceed! Together we facilitated the inaugural Women, Peace and Security training workshop, which was a resounding success. The enthusiasm of the women was breathtaking. They loved learning and soaked up every word. Wanting change, they instinctively knew they were a critical part of that change.

Given the workshop's success, my plan was to refine the training and then roll out the course across the other five geographical sectors in the country. In the short term, the training was designed to encourage and empower the SPLA women to operate more effectively. However, my long-term goal was to reduce sexual violence against the civilian population's women and girls. I wanted to influence the SPLA male commanders whose troops were responsible for committing these atrocities or allowing them to occur. I knew from my gender advisor training that having trained women within a military organisation has a positive impact on that organisation over the long term. Being able to better protect these women and girls was a task worth starting!

The low numbers of uniformed women in the mission was a problem - an impediment to the mission's success. I needed to replicate myself somehow. The mission needed trained military Gender Advisors in the sectors to ensure that a gender perspective was part of all planning and decision-making. There were military Gender Focal Point officers in each of the sectors of the mission. Unfortunately, being a Gender Focal Point was a secondary role and the officer had another primary role. This was not ideal, considering the amount of work that needed to be done in the gender space. Worse still, those military Gender Focal Point officers were not trained in that role! I needed to rectify this situation quickly.

Lieutenant Colonel Rachel Grimes was coming out from New York to conduct a week-long Gender Advisor course in Entebbe, Uganda - right next door! I knew from experience that it would be a great course if Rachel was running it. This was an excellent opportunity to get the Gender Focal Point officers trained. But I needed money! I went cap in hand to the head of the civilian Gender Affairs unit and asked for US$7000 so I could send the six military Gender Focal Point officers and myself to Entebbe for the course. She listened to my pitch and thankfully financed the trip.

Off we went to Entebbe. The six military Gender Focal Point officers were enthusiastic and competent staff officers from many countries, including Rwanda, Nepal and South America. They were all male, except one, as there were so few women in the mission. The course Rachel delivered was first class and my six proteges embraced the well-delivered course content. They immediately understood how they could input gender considerations into their sectors' planning and decision making. I knew they still had limited planning capacity due to their competing primary roles, so I commenced working with UN New York Headquarters to have their six positions changed to make them dedicated full time military Gender Advisors, like myself. Given the mission's priority of protection of civilians and enduring peace, I saw it as critical that we had dedicated military Gender Advisors to influence the planning across the country.

The Gender Advisor course in Uganda was also designed to train future Gender Advisors for UN missions around the world. During the course I was given the task of mentoring those men and women who had been selected to be sent to South Sudan. I told them although the role would be challenging, it would be one of the best jobs they would ever do in the military. A young Ukrainian Army female officer was particularly keen to come to South Sudan, work with me and help the vulnerable people. She was smart, capable, competent and very dedicated - exactly what this young nation needed. She did not know then that she would be needed in her own country a few short years later.

Our Gender Advisor selfie. The Ukranian officer is top right.

On my return to Juba I continued my advocacy with the Senior Military Liaison Officer, who was German. I made sure he knew my mother was German. I would always greet him in my best, and only, German, 'Wie geht es Ihnen heute Morgen, Sir?' (How are you this morning, Sir?) The Commander had 10 women Military Liaison Officers, and there were 10 bases across the country. We needed to double that number. We needed at least 20 women - two women in each location - for safety and mutual support. He agreed wholeheartedly and set to rectify that deficiency. There were 22 women Military Liaison Officers when I left. All were doing an outstanding job and filling the void. Each had the ability to engage with the civilian women. I thanked him profusely for his time and effort. He said, 'We need these women so they can engage with the women in the communities, otherwise we cannot do our job.' This was music to my ears! I knew that commanders like him could lead to much-needed change and progress.

Since the completion of the women's inaugural training, it became clear that they would need ongoing support from each other whilst they went through this period of change. I discovered that UN Police had created a fledgling South Sudanese National Police Service Women's Network - a network that would allow them to provide support to one another. If we joined forces we could help women in both the police and the military. It was a win-win solution.

I made an appointment with the UN Police Commissioner, who happened to be from Fiji. We connected immediately. I talked to her about my time in Fiji during Tropical Cyclone Winston, and my many trips back there to ensure both Australia and Fiji learnt important lessons from TC Winston. I said I always felt as though I was coming home when I flew into Fiji. I recall a colleague saying that he had never met a Fijian he didn't like. I understood what he meant.

The Police Commissioner listened to my plan, liked it, and thankfully said she would help me. She even appointed a dedicated police Gender Advisor who could work with me and who would report back to her on our progress. Great! Now there were two of us! This was a 100 percent increase in uniformed Gender Advisors. The new police Gender Advisor and I set about convincing the UN Development Program to fund and support **both** Women's Networks. They agreed. We were gathering momentum to create real change. I was very impressed with the Police Commissioner - her leadership style plus her courage and conviction were inspirational.

A contingent of UN police - from an African country that had better remain nameless - was deployed to support a township in one of the northern sectors. This police contingent swiftly opened a brothel, taking advantage of the local women. Their actions constituted sexual exploitation and abuse against the population - usually an indication of poor leadership and discipline. The UN and its missions have a zero tolerance of sexual exploitation by its members against the population. Those police were using their power and money to abuse the local women!

As soon as the Police Commissioner found out, she ordered the entire contingent to be thrown out of South Sudan within 48 hours. Her lack of tolerance for sexual exploitation by a trusted, uniformed police contingent against the local population was admirable and very necessary. It is this behaviour by UN forces that can undermine the legitimacy of the mission - indeed all missions. After this incident the mission's leadership had to work extremely hard to restore the population's confidence that it was there to serve and protect.

The Senior Women's Protection Advisor and I received an invitation from the Child Protection Unit to speak to the 10 Generals commanding the SPLA Divisions. It was a Child Protection Workshop conducted with the UN Children's Fund (UNICEF) who were continuing to work towards returning child soldiers to their families. Child soldiers are boys and girls who are recruited against their will and suffer extensive forms of exploitation and abuse. Generally, girls would become 'bush brides' and young boys become soldiers.

The SPLA was keen to be 'delisted' by the UN Headquarters by demonstrating they were no longer abusing human rights. This meant they wanted to become internationally recognised as a professional organisation in their own right and would no longer need to be subject to UN sanctions. By righting the wrongs of the past - by returning the child soldiers - they were demonstrating their professionalism. I was told a lot of the boy child soldiers were returned, but not as many of the girls. Sadly, this did not surprise me.

At the Child Protection Workshop, I used the opportunity to speak to the Generals about the lessons we had learnt in the ADF. I spoke of the importance of understanding the impact of our operations on the population and the importance of having the population on our side at the completion of operations. As a result, the ADF was in the process of creating a Gender Advisor capability. I did not speak about human rights violations - just the operational importance of considering a gender perspective and how this could contribute to mission success.

The questions I received from the Generals indicated they understood the points I was making. Military talk to military. One General said they were having trouble recruiting women into the military. I said, 'Sir, I think you have a retention issue. I know there are hundreds of women already in your military and they simply want to contribute meaningfully to the security of your country alongside the men.' The General nodded and said he would look into it. He already recognised he needed both men and women in his forces. However, he needed to utilise the women already there. Colonel Bol would need Commanders like him to embed enduring change.

The most challenging situation I had to deal with was hearing that a 10-year-old girl had been imprisoned for adultery. I knew about the poor conditions of the prisons. The prisoners were manacled at the ankles - a situation I would not wish on anyone, let alone an innocent little girl who had been raped then sent to prison for adultery! There was a frightening amount of freedom from punishment for the perpetrators of sexual violence, due to the breakdown of the judicial system where the society and culture favoured the male. A lot needed to change to achieve peace and justice for these women and girls.

The Deputy Commander called me into his office to talk about a problem he had heard concerning local women and girls suffering from obstetric fistula. He wanted me to help. I was impressed he was now taking an interest in the plight of local vulnerable women and girls.

A currently serving female SPLA soldier

Obstetric fistula usually occurs in young girls during childbirth. Due to their narrow hips, the difficult birth can cause the baby's head to sit against the wall of the uterus for extended periods. This kills the muscle and tears holes in the birthing canal, the bladder and the anal canal. The girls and women then leak urine and faeces. This ostracises them from their communities and robs them of their ability to make a living. They become the most vulnerable of the vulnerable!

The only solution is complex surgery and after-surgery care. In most cases the patients require nutritional support prior to the surgery, as they are malnourished due to the condition.

There are many root causes of obstetric fistula. Sexual and gender-based violence was rife throughout South Sudan. It was a very poor country. After a long drawn out conflict, drought and famine, the bride price had escalated. Families would sell their daughters at a young age in order to receive the bride price. Bride price is usually paid in cows. This in turn contributes to the continual violence in the community as pastoralists and cattle herders not only compete for the same land, but cattle theft is rife. Men steal cattle so they can pay the exorbitant bride price. A vicious circle!

There were approximately 60,000 known cases of obstetric fistula in South Sudan alone. The plan was that we would initially focus on at least 50 women and girls - the youngest being 10. I understood why the Deputy Commander thought this task was worthy of receiving resources.

I spoke to the head of the UN Population Fund (UNFPA), who happened to be an Australian. I had struck up a good working relationship with her in regards to gender based violence reporting. UNFPA was responsible for working with the South Sudanese government to bring surgical specialists from across Africa to conduct surgery on women and girls with obstetric fistula. My job was to identify and bring the selected patients back to Juba for surgery. I worked with civilian-military planners, as they had the manpower and the boots on the ground in the sectors to find these deserving patients. Without the interest of the Deputy Commander, these unfortunate people would have continued their difficult lives and been forever marginalised from their families and society. To us it seemed an obvious solution, but to those women and girls it meant a whole new future opening up to them. It was really life-changing for the fortunate few - but only scratched the surface of this mammoth global problem.

17 – INVESTMENT IN CHANGE

I learnt on the Nordic Training Centre Gender Advisor course that statistics state that if you gave money or aid to the man in a family, he would give 10% to the family and spend the rest on himself - smoking, drinking, gambling etc. If you gave the same money to the woman, she may spend 10% on herself and the rest would go to the family for food, education and the other necessities of life. I wanted to test this theory in South Sudan.

I selected five women whom I had met - all from different backgrounds - and gave each one US$100. While they were initially ecstatic, they were sobered by the responsibility for spending such a large amount of money. I had asked them to come back and tell me how they had used the money. One woman told me she spent it on food, more rice and meat for her children to help them concentrate at school. Another woman spent it on school fees, school uniforms and food for the family. Two spent their money on improving their businesses so they could provide more money for their families. It allowed one woman to return to Entebbe to support her family at a funeral, which she otherwise could not have afforded. She was even able to buy a dress for the funeral. In all cases the women spent the money to improve the life and education of their families. Women do put their families first! Mum had demonstrated that her entire life. This is a fact that needs to be considered when managing aid to any country.

We were visited by the Defence Attaché from the Australian Embassy in Ethiopia and a Foreign Affairs political officer who was representing the Australian Ambassador in meetings with the South Sudanese Government. The political officer was particularly interested in efforts within the mission to progress gender and child protection issues. As the mission's Military Gender Advisor, it was my job to accompany her to numerous meetings and briefings.

I introduced her to key people such as the Women's Protection Officer and the head of the Child Protection Unit. He was from Uganda, and had been a child soldier himself. Extremely experienced and capable, he was working with the SPLA leadership, conducting workshops similar to the one I had been asked to address. During this meeting they discussed how Australia could contribute to building schools in South Sudan. This was the first time I had seen how Australian aid is allocated. The Child Protection Unit already had a prioritised list of where schools needed to be built - where the need and the impact was the greatest. I felt comfortable that our aid would be targeted and well spent. Those schools would make a great change in the lives of those girls and boys.

After the visit from the Australian Embassy officials, I went back to work on my never-ending list of tasks - those that would create change and could be handed over to my replacement shortly. A week later, I was called into the Australian Commander's office. The Australian Defence Attaché had contacted him to say that the political officer had been impressed with my leadership and initiative to progress women and child protection under such challenging political and security conditions. She wanted me to share my experiences and lessons learnt with other African states after I finished my tour. Unfortunately, I was on contract, which did not allow me time to spend at the Australian Embassy in Ethiopia on my way home. I was quite chuffed, however, to hear that the political officer recognised the impact Gender Advisors can make in UN missions.

Out and about gender advising

As I was nearing the end of my tour of duty, I told my Commander that I believed the Military Gender Advisor role was critical to the mission's planning and decision-making. In my short nine months I had focused on training the women within the South Sudanese security forces, empowering them to contribute to the security of their country, and in the long term, reducing sexual violence against the population. It was the security force's role to provide a safe and secure environment, where sexual violence is prevented and vulnerable people are protected. To ensure the work I had started was continued, I wrote detailed handover notes to my successor. When asked what I remembered the most about my tour I wrote:

"The fatigue and tiredness on the faces of the Sudanese Peace Liberation Army (SPLA) women who have been fighting for over 20 years and all they want is peace. Yet there is no peace, there is no pension, some of them don't even have a roof over their heads! The UNMISS civilian and military components need to consider the implications of demobilisation of women in the national security forces. Well, consider women - period!"

I then wrote a formal Post Activity Report which is commented on by my Commander before it is sent back to Joint Operations Command for consideration in future Gender Advisor deployments. He wrote the following comments on my Post Activity Report:

"Given the nature of this Civil War, and history of deeply embedded gender and child violence in this country, there remains significant potential to progress these issues. In a UN Mission that is treading water on much of its mandate, Lieutenant Colonel Fellowes has adopted a novel approach in actively engaging government forces to generate change from within. The Republic of South Sudan Military possess much

*power in this country, and Lieutenant Colonel Fellowes' efforts to shape and influence senior SPLA officers has potential to achieve **sustainable** change."*

It was great to see that the Commander had understood what I was trying to achieve. Change from within any organisation takes time. In the world's newest nation, it had been my responsibility to try to assist those women - to empower them so they could make their own change and secure their own equality and futures.

In September 2018 it was time to return home after the most challenging yet rewarding job I had ever done. I was at Juba airport on the way home. I had googled that Juba was voted the worst International Airport in the world, and that was certainly true. The airport lounge was either a tree or, if you were lucky, a World Food Program tent.

I was sitting under a tree waiting for my plane back to Uganda when I saw a woman cutting the grass with a small knife between the 'lounge' and the tarmac. I still had several hundred dollars worth of South Sudanese Pounds. When we were called onto our flight, I stayed back so the other passengers were ahead of me. I walked up to this woman, greeted her and slipped her the money. I said, 'Thank you for everything you have done and everything you are going to do.' She had an absolutely incredulous expression on her face. This was the last thing she thought would happen to her that day. She said, 'Thank you, thank you, thank you, madam,' with tears welling up in her eyes. We just stared at each other in wordless communication. I turned and walked onto the plane - tears in my eyes too. From my seat on the plane I could still see her - a tiny figure, standing there, staring at the plane, her hands clutched in front of her chest. One thing I knew for sure was this woman would use the money wisely for the good of her family and her community.

Future agents of change

In the nine months I had been there, I could see change was slowly underway. People like Colonel Bol, with the assistance of the Women's Protection Officer, the heads of Gender Affairs and the Child Protection Unit, were all striving to improve the lives of women and children in South Sudan. I left South Sudan physically and mentally spent. I had invested everything I had to give. I had made sure I focused on making sustainable change and it was now up to these women to be their **own** agents of change - to fly with their **own** wings.

18 – BAD CHANGE, GOOD CHANGE

My experience in South Sudan demonstrated how complex, wicked problems can keep a country from achieving the peace and prosperity it deserves. The lesson I had learnt over and over again was that women were pivotal to long term peace and they were capable of being the agents of change their country needed.

Back in Australia, after a break of several months, I started work as a Contingency Planning Officer at Headquarters 1st Division in Brisbane. I was very happy to work in Brisbane, only two hours from home. I had been away from home for four years - Afghanistan, Canberra and South Sudan. My focus now turned to the South West Pacific.

In May 2021 President Biden announced US forces were withdrawing from Afghanistan. Suddenly, the entire Headquarters' focus changed back to Afghanistan. By mid-August, the startling capitulation of Afghan security forces and the collapse of the central government to the Taliban was complete. It was heartbreaking to watch the ensuing terror and confusion in Kabul - as men, women, girls and boys tried to flee the country to safety.

The largest ever non-combatant evacuation was activated, including planners from our Headquarters, deploying to Kabul. We were glued to the TV watching the first planes fill up with the strongest people - all men and boys - who could push to the front of the waiting crowds outside Hamid Karzai

International Airport. Women and children, the weaker and smaller, were being pushed to the back of the huge determined crowds.

As I watched the carnage unfold, suddenly my ears start to ring loudly and I felt the familiar weight of my pistol resting on my hip. I had worn a pistol every day in Afghanistan for self-protection. I reached down to check it. Of course it wasn't there. For a moment I was back in Kabul. I shook my head at the weirdness of the feeling. All I could think about was the plight of those women and children who would be left behind. All the work and change that had been done over the last twenty years had been undone in an instant! I also felt for the women who were trained in their security forces - the Taliban would not accept them in that role.

There are reports that the Taliban are actively hunting and killing the women who had served in the police and army. A terrifying change! This was a devastating blow to my colleagues Amanda Fielding and Dee Gibbon, who had been tasked with ensuring women were recruited and trained into these organisations. Understandably they have both suffered mental anguish as, one by one, they no longer hear from those Afghan women – those women who received a death sentence for trying to change their country! Amanda has discharged from the Army and Dee has retired from full time duty. Another bad change!

Senior Gender Advisor, Group Captain Dee Gibbon, working closely with a local community in Kabul, 2016

The Taliban said they would uphold the rights of women, but of course they did not. Almost immediately a ban was placed on women leaving their homes without a male guardian. Women now needed a male relative to join them for basic tasks such as entering government buildings, seeing a doctor or catching a taxi. The Taliban reneged on their promise to open schools for girls over sixth grade. The inability of women to move around freely hindered them from accessing their basic human rights. Women who went out without a male relative were harassed, stopped, detained and blocked from doing the things they were trying to do. Women vanished from politics. Most women civil servants, who previously made up a quarter of all staff, were told to stay at home indefinitely. Many women were simply too scared to venture outdoors. And the worst was yet to come.

The Taliban announced their Decree that **all** women need to wear a head-to-toe burka as it is 'traditional and respectful'. The Decree goes on to say that if women had no important work outside it was 'better they stay at home'. With a snap of the fingers the Taliban wiped the country's access to 50% of the population! This country and its future will be infinitely poorer for making this change.

Like many people who worked in Afghanistan, I have been heartbroken and devastated to watch the evacuation and then the swift decapitation of women's rights. I cannot understand why President Biden did not gradually withdraw his forces, making sure the Afghanistan security forces filled the void and had the capability and capacity to secure their country. His decisions thrust the most vulnerable people under the bus! Young girls are now forced to marry. Girls are being sold to pay for food for the family. Girls are being denied education and medical help. I do not know what the future holds for these women and girls, but I do believe it was totally preventable!

I recently saw an Afghan woman being interviewed on TV about the changes enforced by the Taliban. Naturally her face was obscured to protect her identity. She said it seemed that all the work done over the last 20 years had been in vain. She felt that her wings had been **broken off!** A very bad change.

On another front, the Ukrainian Gender Advisor I had trained with in Africa reached out to our Gender Advisor Network for help after the Russian invasion of Ukraine. She needed assistance to buy a car so her team, all trained psychologists, could move into the regions worst hit by the Russian invasion. Ukrainian civilians, men, women, girls and boys were suffering conflict-related sexual violence and torture. Once again, the vulnerable population were being targeted. Rape was still being used as a weapon of war. History was repeating itself.

The Gender Advisor was able to raise the money for the car and her team headed to where they were most needed. She was killed in a Russian attack shortly after. However, it took three weeks for us to hear the terrible news. I was shocked and saddened. What a waste of human life. She had been killed trying to help those in most need. May she rest in peace.

I was not always successful in creating change. However, it has been pleasing to see the maturation of the ADF. Women are now serving alongside their male counterparts in all combat related roles. Our differences are our strength, and should continue to be embraced. I hear policy has been introduced to provide women who are Commanding Officers with financial assistance for home help (au pairs etc) to enable them to compete equitably with their male peers and also have a family. A good change.

The UN have focused on increasing the number of trained women in its missions. History has repeatedly shown that engagement with the vulnerable population - women, children, the elderly and handicapped - is the first to be pushed aside in the rush to resolve conflict. The focus is on obtaining peace as quickly as possible - peace at **any** price.

Engagement with those most affected by the conflict does not occur. The vulnerable population know what they need and they need to be asked. Military forces need to contain trained personnel, including women, so they can engage with and support the whole population.

Deb Warren-Smith, now a civilian working in New York with UN Women, told me the UN has developed the concept of an Engagement Platoon - half men and half women - and piloted their training. This is wonderful news and will allow the deliberate engagement with women in conflict and post conflict settings. This in turn, means better, more inclusive solutions for the vulnerable population. A good change.

Any meaningful, long term change requires **both** men and women to contribute. This always results in longer term peace and prosperity. Empirical evidence states that if women are involved in the peace process, the resulting agreement is 35% more likely to last at least 15 years *(International Peace Institute)*. Engaging women as part of the peace process is no longer optional, it is **critical!**

19 - FUTURE CHANGE

I know I said at the start that my story begins and ends with me living in a beautiful part of Australia, in Ravensbourne. However, my story isn't likely to end here. I took a break from the Army this year so I could spend my days, when not writing this book, reflecting on my life journey and seeking clarity about what I want to do next. What is my next chapter of change?

I know I will always feel restless when there is ongoing injustice for women in conflict zones around the world. The Army trained me to the pinnacle of a Green Beret, and if I have the skills, knowledge and committment, I feel like it will be hard not to answer the call.

Having lived just over half a century on this earth, my future is still full of possibilities. I know that I want a life that brings me peace. This is why I named my property 'Hakuna Matata' which means 'Peaceful' in Swahili or of course 'No worries' in the movie the Lion King. I look out at the trees around my house and reflect how trees have protected and affected me. Climbing trees to escape domestic violence as a child - contemplating ending my life at the 'Death Tree' – sitting under a tree in South Sudan after an exhausting tour of duty and reflecting on the importance of women's influence. Trees always fill me with peace. I know I am not yet feeling peace in every moment, of every day, but I am on that spiritual journey.

I have also started my health journey as my body succumbs to severe osteoarthritis from injuries sustained during my military service. I walk with a limp - bilateral knee replacements and ankle fusions are closer to happening than I would like. I have started the long rehabilitation road. I call it my Best Year of Health Ever - achieving my best mental and physical health in the next 12 months - being the best version of myself.

So, what's next for me? I am in the fortunate position of having a number of options, all of which I am considering. I could remain attached to the Army and undertake more reserve work, in the field of humanitarian assistance or the gender focussed work that I enjoy so much. I could resume my health business, which was highly successful before I rejoined the full-time Army in 2015. I could spend endless happy hours maintaining my property, keeping the weeds out of my vegetable garden and orchard. I could also forge an entirely new path, perhaps volunteering my time to helping women just like my mum escape from violent situations. These are all good options, and my many years in the Army have made it possible for me to have the luxury of choice.

Wherever my path takes me next, I know that I will always be a good friend, sister, mate, role model and, of course, daughter. Although Mum is no longer on this earth, I will always strive to make her proud of the person I have become. As I stated in the beginning, I wrote this book to honour my Mother's memory and I know that she would be proud of me for telling my story with a view to helping others in similar situations. I still miss her every day and, in every way, but telling my story has definitely been cathartic.

Mum taught me that we can overcome any adversity – that we all have strength and confidence to make whatever change we wish. She gave me the wings of change.

Mission accomplished!

www.ingramcontent.com/pod-product-compliance
Lightning Source LLC
Chambersburg PA
CBHW070258010526
44107CB00056B/2496